NOTES OF A WAR CORRESPONDENT

Richard Harding Davis

Notes of a War Correspondent

R. H. Davis

© 1st World Library – Literary Society, 2004
PO Box 2211
Fairfield, IA 52556
www.1stworldlibrary.org
First Edition

LCCN: 2003099793

ISBN: 1-59540-115-6

Purchase *"Notes of a War Correspondent"*
as a traditional bound book at:
www.1stWorldLibrary.org/purchase.asp?ISBN=1-59540-115-6

1st World Library Literary Society is a nonprofit organization dedicated to promoting literacy by:

- Creating a free internet library accessible from any computer worldwide.
- Hosting writing competitions and offering book publishing scholarships.

Readers interested in supporting literacy through sponsorship, donations or membership please contact:
literacy@1stworldlibrary.org
Check us out at: www.1stworldlibrary.org

Notes of a War Correspondent
*contributed by Ed, Tim & Rodney
in support of
1st World Library Literary Society*

Contents:

The Cuban-Spanish War
   The Death of Rodriguez............................ 7

The Greek-Turkish War
   The Battle of Velestinos...........................16

The Spanish-American War
   I.   The Rough Riders at Guasimas................ 34
   II. The Battle of San Juan Hill...................... 58
   III. The Taking of Coamo............................... 75
   IV. The Passing of San Juan Hill.................. 84

The South African War
   I.   With Buller's Column............................. 100
   II. The Relief of Ladysmith......................... 116
   III. The Night Before the Battle...................133

The Japanese-Russian War
   Battles I did not see...............................151

A War Correspondent's Kit............................168

Footnotes..186

THE CUBAN-SPANISH WAR:

THE DEATH OF RODRIGUEZ {1}

Adolfo Rodriguez was the only son of a Cuban farmer, who lived nine miles outside of Santa Clara, beyond the hills that surround that city to the north.

When the revolution in Cuba broke out young Rodriguez joined the insurgents, leaving his father and mother and two sisters at the farm. He was taken, in December of 1896, by a force of the Guardia Civile, the corps d'elite of the Spanish army, and defended himself when they tried to capture him, wounding three of them with his machete.

He was tried by a military court for bearing arms against the government, and sentenced to be shot by a fusillade some morning before sunrise.

Previous to execution he was confined in the military prison of Santa Clara with thirty other insurgents, all of whom were sentenced to be shot, one after the other, on mornings following the execution of Rodriguez.

His execution took place the morning of the 19th of January, 1897, at a place a half-mile distant from the city, on the great plain that stretches from the forts out to the hills, beyond which Rodriguez had lived for nineteen years. At the time of his death he was twenty years old.

I witnessed his execution, and what follows is an account of the way he went to his death. The young man's friends could not be present, for it was impossible for them to show themselves in that crowd and that place with wisdom or without distress, and I like to think that, although Rodriguez could not know it, there was one person present when he died who felt keenly for him, and who was a sympathetic though unwilling spectator.

There had been a full moon the night preceding the execution, and when the squad of soldiers marched from town it was still shining brightly through the mists. It lighted a plain two miles in extent, broken by ridges and gullies and covered with thick, high grass, and with bunches of cactus and palmetto. In the hollow of the ridges the mist lay like broad lakes of water, and on one side of the plain stood the walls of the old town. On the other rose hills covered with royal palms that showed white in the moonlight, like hundreds of marble columns. A line of tiny camp-fires that the sentries had built during the night stretched between the forts at regular intervals and burned clearly.

But as the light grew stronger and the moonlight faded these were stamped out, and when the soldiers came in force the moon was a white ball in the sky, without radiance, the fires had sunk to ashes, and the sun had not yet risen.

So even when the men were formed into three sides of a hollow square, they were scarcely able to distinguish one another in the uncertain light of the morning.

There were about three hundred soldiers in the formation. They belonged to the volunteers, and they deployed upon the plain with their band in front playing a jaunty quickstep, while their officers galloped from one side to the other through the grass, seeking a suitable place for the execution. Outside the line the band still played merrily.

A few men and boys, who had been dragged out of their beds by the music, moved about the ridges behind the soldiers, half-clothed, unshaven, sleepy-eyed, yawning, stretching themselves nervously and shivering in the cool, damp air of the morning.

Either owing to discipline or on account of the nature of their errand, or because the men were still but half awake, there was no talking in the ranks, and the soldiers stood motionless, leaning on their rifles, with their backs turned to the town, looking out across the plain to the hills.

The men in the crowd behind them were also grimly silent. They knew that whatever they might say would be twisted into a word of sympathy for the condemned man or a protest against the government. So no one spoke; even the officers gave their orders in gruff whispers, and the men in the crowd did not mix together, but looked suspiciously at one another and kept apart.

As the light increased a mass of people came hurrying from the town with two black figures leading them, and the soldiers drew up at attention, and part of the double line fell back and left an opening in the square.

With us a condemned man walks only the short

distance from his cell to the scaffold or the electric chair, shielded from sight by the prison walls, and it often occurs even then that the short journey is too much for his strength and courage.

But the Spaniards on this morning made the prisoner walk for over a half-mile across the broken surface of the fields. I expected to find the man, no matter what his strength at other times might be, stumbling and faltering on this cruel journey; but as he came nearer I saw that he led all the others, that the priests on either side of him were taking two steps to his one, and that they were tripping on their gowns and stumbling over the hollows in their efforts to keep pace with him as he walked, erect and soldierly, at a quick step in advance of them.

He had a handsome, gentle face of the peasant type, a light, pointed beard, great wistful eyes, and a mass of curly black hair. He was shockingly young for such a sacrifice, and looked more like a Neapolitan than a Cuban. You could imagine him sitting on the quay at Naples or Genoa lolling in the sun and showing his white teeth when he laughed. Around his neck, hanging outside his linen blouse, he wore a new scapular.

It seems a petty thing to have been pleased with at such a time, but I confess to have felt a thrill of satisfaction when I saw, as the Cuban passed me, that he held a cigarette between his lips, not arrogantly nor with bravado, but with the nonchalance of a man who meets his punishment fearlessly, and who will let his enemies see that they can kill but cannot frighten him.

It was very quickly finished, with rough and, but for

one frightful blunder, with merciful swiftness. The crowd fell back when it came to the square, and the condemned man, the priests, and the firing squad of six young volunteers passed in and the line closed behind them.

The officer who had held the cord that bound the Cuban's arms behind him and passed across his breast, let it fall on the grass and drew his sword, and Rodriguez dropped his cigarette from his lips and bent and kissed the cross which the priest held up before him.

The elder of the priests moved to one side and prayed rapidly in a loud whisper, while the other, a younger man, walked behind the firing squad and covered his face with his hands. They had both spent the last twelve hours with Rodriguez in the chapel of the prison.

The Cuban walked to where the officer directed him to stand, and turning his back on the square, faced the hills and the road across them, which led to his father's farm.

As the officer gave the first command he straightened himself as far as the cords would allow, and held up his head and fixed his eyes immovably on the morning light, which had just begun to show above the hills.

He made a picture of such pathetic helplessness, but of such courage and dignity, that he reminded me on the instant of that statue of Nathan Hale which stands in the City Hall Park, above the roar of Broadway. The Cuban's arms were bound, as are those of the statue, and he stood firmly, with his weight resting on his heels like a soldier on parade, and with his face held up fearlessly, as is that of the statue. But there was this difference, that Rodriguez, while probably as willing to give six lives for his country as was the American rebel, being only a peasant, did not think to say so, and he will not, in consequence, live in bronze during the lives of many men, but will be remembered only as one of thirty Cubans, one of whom was shot at Santa Clara on each succeeding day at sunrise.

The officer had given the order, the men had raised their pieces, and the condemned man had heard the clicks of the triggers as they were pulled back, and he had not moved. And then happened one of the most cruelly refined, though unintentional, acts of torture that one can very well imagine. As the officer slowly raised his sword, preparatory to giving the signal, one of the mounted officers rode up to him and pointed out silently that, as I had already observed with some satisfaction, the firing squad were so placed that when they fired they would shoot several of the soldiers stationed on the extreme end of the square.

Their captain motioned his men to lower their pieces, and then walked across the grass and laid his hand on the shoulder of the waiting prisoner.

It is not pleasant to think what that shock must have been. The man had steeled himself to receive a volley of bullets. He believed that in the next instant he would be in another world; he had heard the command given, had heard the click of the Mausers as the locks caught - and then, at that supreme moment, a human hand had been laid upon his shoulder and a voice spoke in his ear.

You would expect that any man, snatched back to life in such a fashion would start and tremble at the reprieve, or would break down altogether, but this boy turned his head steadily, and followed with his eyes the direction of the officer's sword, then nodded gravely, and, with his shoulders squared, took up the new position, straightened his back, and once more held himself erect.

As an exhibition of self-control this should surely rank above feats of heroism performed in battle, where there are thousands of comrades to give inspiration. This man was alone, in sight of the hills he knew, with only enemies about him, with no source to draw on for strength but that which lay within himself.

The officer of the firing squad, mortified by his blunder, hastily whipped up his sword, the men once more levelled their rifles, the sword rose, dropped, and the men fired. At the report the Cuban's head snapped back almost between his shoulders, but his body fell slowly, as though some one had pushed him gently forward from behind and he had stumbled.

He sank on his side in the wet grass without a struggle or sound, and did not move again.

It was difficult to believe that he meant to lie there, that it could be ended so without a word, that the man in the linen suit would not rise to his feet and continue to walk on over the hills, as he apparently had started to do, to his home; that there was not a mistake somewhere, or that at least some one would be sorry or say something or run to pick him up.

But, fortunately, he did not need help, and the priests

returned - the younger one with the tears running down his face - and donned their vestments and read a brief requiem for his soul, while the squad stood uncovered, and the men in hollow square shook their accoutrements into place, and shifted their pieces and got ready for the order to march, and the band began again with the same quickstep which the fusillade had interrupted.

The figure still lay on the grass untouched, and no one seemed to remember that it had walked there of itself, or noticed that the cigarette still burned, a tiny ring of living fire, at the place where the figure had first stood.

The figure was a thing of the past, and the squad shook itself like a great snake, and then broke into little pieces and started off jauntily, stumbling in the high grass and striving to keep step to the music.

The officers led it past the figure in the linen suit, and so close to it that the file closers had to part with the column to avoid treading on it. Each soldier as he passed turned and looked down on it, some craning their necks curiously, others giving a careless glance, and some without any interest at all, as they would have looked at a house by the roadside, or a hole in the road.

One young soldier caught his foot in a trailing vine, just opposite to it, and fell. He grew very red when his comrades giggled at him for his awkwardness. The crowd of sleepy spectators fell in on either side of the band. They, too, had forgotten it, and the priests put their vestments back in the bag and wrapped their heavy cloaks about them, and hurried off after the others.

Every one seemed to have forgotten it except two men, who came slowly towards it from the town, driving a bullock-cart that bore an unplaned coffin, each with a cigarette between his lips, and with his throat wrapped in a shawl to keep out the morning mists.

At that moment the sun, which had shown some promise of its coming in the glow above the hills, shot up suddenly from behind them in all the splendor of the tropics, a fierce, red disk of heat, and filled the air with warmth and light.

The bayonets of the retreating column flashed in it, and at the sight a rooster in a farm-yard near by crowed vigorously, and a dozen bugles answered the challenge with the brisk, cheery notes of the reveille, and from all parts of the city the church bells jangled out the call for early mass, and the little world of Santa Clara seemed to stretch itself and to wake to welcome the day just begun.

But as I fell in at the rear of the procession and looked back, the figure of the young Cuban, who was no longer a part of the world of Santa Clara, was asleep in the wet grass, with his motionless arms still tightly bound behind him, with the scapular twisted awry across his face, and the blood from his breast sinking into the soil he had tried to free.

THE GREEK-TURKISH WAR:

THE BATTLE OF VELESTINOS {2}

The Turks had made three attacks on Velestinos on three different days, and each time had been repulsed. A week later, on the 4th of May, they came back again, to the number of ten thousand, and brought four batteries with them, and the fighting continued for two more days. This was called the second battle of Velestinos. In the afternoon of the 5th the Crown Prince withdrew from Pharsala to take up a stronger position at Domokos, and the Greeks under General Smolenski, the military hero of the campaign, were forced to retreat, and the Turks came in, and, according to their quaint custom, burned the village and marched on to Volo. John Bass, the American correspondent, and myself were keeping house in the village, in the home of the mayor. He had fled from the town, as had nearly all the villagers; and as we liked the appearance of his house, I gave Bass a leg up over the wall around his garden, and Bass opened the gate, and we climbed in through his front window. It was like the invasion of the home of the Dusantes by Mrs. Lecks and Mrs. Aleshine, and, like them, we were constantly making discoveries of fresh treasure-trove. Sometimes it was in the form of a cake of soap or a tin of coffee, and once it was the mayor's fluted petticoats, which we tried on, and found very heavy. We could not discover what he did for pockets. All of these things, and the house itself, were burned to ashes, we were told, a few hours after we retreated, and we feel less troubled now at having made such free use of them.

On the morning of the 4th we were awakened by the firing of cannon from a hill just over our heads, and we met in the middle of the room and solemnly shook hands. There was to be a battle, and we were the only correspondents on the spot. As I represented the London Times, Bass was the only representative of an American newspaper who saw this fight from its beginning to its end.

We found all the hills to the left of the town topped with long lines of men crouching in little trenches. There were four rows of hills. If you had measured the distance from one hill-top to the next, they would have been from one hundred to three hundred yards distant from one another. In between the hills were gullies, or little valleys, and the beds of streams that had dried up in the hot sun. These valleys were filled with high grass that waved about in the breeze and was occasionally torn up and tossed in the air by a shell. The position of the Greek forces was very simple. On the top of each hill was a trench two or three feet deep and some hundred yards long. The earth that had been scooped out to make the trench was packed on the edge facing the enemy, and on the top of that some of the men had piled stones, through which they poked their rifles. When a shell struck the ridge it would sometimes scatter these stones in among the men, and they did quite as much damage as the shells. Back of these trenches, and down that side of the hill which was farther from the enemy, were the reserves, who sprawled at length in the long grass, and smoked and talked and watched the shells dropping into the gully at their feet.

The battle, which lasted two days, opened in a sudden and terrific storm of hail. But the storm passed as quickly as it came, leaving the trenches running with water, like the gutters of a city street after a spring shower; and the men soon sopped them up with their overcoats and blankets, and in half an hour the sun had dried the wet uniforms, and the field-birds had begun to chirp again, and the grass was warm and fragrant. The sun was terribly hot. There was no other day during that entire brief campaign when its glare was so intense or the heat so suffocating. The men curled up in the trenches, with their heads pressed against the damp earth, panting and breathing heavily, and the heat-waves danced and quivered about them, making the plain below flicker like a picture in a cinematograph.

From time to time an officer would rise and peer down into the great plain, shading his eyes with his hands, and shout something at them, and they would turn quickly in the trench and rise on one knee. And at the shout that followed they would fire four or five rounds rapidly and evenly, and then, at a sound from the officer's whistle, would drop back again and pick up the cigarettes they had placed in the grass and begin leisurely to swab out their rifles with a piece of dirty rag on a cleaning rod. Down in the plain below there was apparently nothing at which they could shoot except the great shadows of the clouds drifting across the vast checker-board of green and yellow fields, and disappearing finally between the mountain passes beyond. In some places there were square dark patches that might have been bushes, and nearer to us than these were long lines of fresh earth, from which steam seemed to be escaping in little wisps. What impressed us most of what we could see of the battle then was the remarkable number of cartridges the Greek soldiers wasted in firing into space, and the fact that they had begun to fire at such long range that, in order to get the elevation, they had placed the rifle butt under the armpit instead of against the shoulder. Their sights were at the top notch. The cartridges reminded one of corn-cobs jumping out of a corn-sheller, and it was interesting when the bolts were shot back to see a hundred of them pop up into the air at the same time, flashing in the sun as though they were glad to have done their work and to get out again. They rolled by the dozens underfoot, and twinkled in the grass, and when one shifted his position in the narrow trench, or stretched his cramped legs, they tinkled musically. It was like wading in a gutter filled with thimbles.

Then there began a concert which came from just overhead - a concert of jarring sounds and little whispers. The "shrieking shrapnel," of which one reads in the description of every battle, did not seem so much like a shriek as it did like the jarring sound of telegraph wires when some one strikes the pole from which they hang, and when they came very close the noise was like the rushing sound that rises between two railroad trains when they pass each other in opposite directions and at great speed. After a few hours we learned by observation that when a shell sang overhead it had already struck somewhere else, which was comforting, and which was explained, of course, by the fact that the speed of the shell is so much greater than the rate at which sound travels. The bullets were much more disturbing; they seemed to be less open in their warfare, and to steal up and sneak by, leaving no sign, and only to whisper as they passed. They moved under a cloak of invisibility, and made one feel as though he were the blind man in a game of blind-man's-buff, where every one tapped him in passing, leaving him puzzled and ignorant as to whither they had gone and from what point they would come next. The bullets sounded like rustling silk, or like humming-birds on a warm summer's day, or like the wind as it is imitated on the stage of a theatre. Any one who has stood behind the scenes when a storm is progressing on the stage, knows the little wheel wound with silk that brushes against another piece of silk, and which produces the whistling effect of the wind. At Velestinos, when the firing was very heavy, it was exactly as though some one were turning one of these silk wheels, and so rapidly as to make the whistling continuous.

When this concert opened, the officers shouted out new orders, and each of the men shoved his sight nearer to the barrel, and when he fired again, rubbed the butt of his gun snugly against his shoulder. The huge green blotches on the plain had turned blue, and now we could distinguish that they moved, and that they were moving steadily forward. Then they would cease to move, and a little later would be hidden behind great puffs of white smoke, which were followed by a flash of flame; and still later there would come a dull report. At the same instant something would hurl itself jarring through the air above our heads, and by turning on one elbow we could see a sudden upheaval in the sunny landscape behind us, a spurt of earth and stones like a miniature geyser, which was filled with broken branches and tufts of grass and pieces of rock. As the Turkish aim grew better these volcanoes appeared higher up the hill, creeping nearer and nearer to the rampart of fresh earth on the second trench until the shells hammered it at last again and again, sweeping it away and cutting great gashes in it, through which we saw the figures of men caught up and hurled to one side, and others flinging themselves face downward as though they were diving into water; and at the same instant in our own trench the men would gasp as though they had been struck too, and then becoming conscious of having done this would turn and smile sheepishly at each other, and crawl closer into the burrows they had made in the earth.

From where we sat on the edge of the trench, with our feet among the cartridges, we could, by leaning forward, look over the piled-up earth into the plain below, and soon, without any aid from field-glasses, we saw the blocks of blue break up into groups of men. These men came across the ploughed fields in long, widely opened lines, walking easily and leisurely, as though they were playing golf or sowing seed in the furrows.

The Greek rifles crackled and flashed at the lines, but the men below came on quite steadily, picking their way over the furrows and appearing utterly unconscious of the seven thousand rifles that were calling on them to halt. They were advancing directly toward a little sugar-loaf hill, on the top of which was a mountain battery perched like a tiara on a woman's head. It was throwing one shell after another in the very path of the men below, but the Turks still continued to pick their way across the field, without showing any regard for the mountain battery. It was worse than threatening; it seemed almost as though they meant to insult us. If they had come up on a run they would not have appeared so contemptuous, for it would have looked then as though they were trying to escape the Greek fire, or that they were at least interested in what was going forward. But the steady advance of so many men, each plodding along by himself, with his head bowed and his gun on his shoulder, was aggravating.

There was a little village at the foot of the hill. It was so small that no one had considered it. It was more like a collection of stables gathered round a residence than a town, and there was a wall completely encircling it, with a gate in the wall that faced us. Suddenly the doors of this gate were burst open from the inside, and a man in a fez ran through them, followed by many more. The first man was waving a sword, and a peasant in petticoats ran at his side and pointed up with his hand at our trench. Until that moment the battle had lacked all human interest; we might have been watching a fight against the stars or the man in the moon, and, in spite of the noise and clatter of the Greek rifles, and the ghostlike whispers and the rushing sounds in the air, there was nothing to remind us of any other battle of which we had heard or read. But we had seen pictures of officers waving swords, and we knew that the fez was the sign of the Turk - of the enemy - of the men who were invading Thessaly, who were at that moment planning to come up a steep hill on which we happened to be sitting and attack the people on top of it. And the spectacle at once became comprehensible, and took on the human interest it had lacked. The men seemed to feel this, for they sprang up and began cheering and shouting, and fired in an upright position, and by so doing exposed themselves at full length to the fire from the men below. The Turks in front of the village ran back into it again, and those in the fields beyond turned and began to move away, but in that same plodding, aggravating fashion. They moved so leisurely that there was a pause in the noise along the line, while the men watched them to make sure that they were really retreating. And then there was a long cheer, after which they all sat down, breathing deeply, and wiping the sweat and dust across their faces, and took long pulls at their canteens.

The different trenches were not all engaged at the same time. They acted according to the individual judgment of their commanding officer, but always for the general good. Sometimes the fire of the enemy would be directed on one particular trench, and it would be impossible for the men in that trench to rise and reply without having their heads carried away; so they would lie hidden, and the men in the trenches flanking them would act in their behalf, and rake the enemy from the front and from every side, until the fire on that trench was silenced, or turned upon some other point. The trenches stretched for over half a mile in a semicircle, and the little hills over which they ran lay at so many different angles, and rose to such different heights, that sometimes the men in one trench fired directly over the heads of their own men. From many trenches in the first line it was impossible to see any of the Greek soldiers except those immediately beside you. If you looked back or beyond on either hand there was nothing to be seen but high hills topped with fresh earth, and the waving yellow grass, and the glaring blue sky.

General Smolenski directed the Greeks from the plain to the far right of the town; and his presence there, although none of the men saw nor heard of him directly throughout the entire day, was more potent for good than would have been the presence of five thousand other men held in reserve. He was a mile or two miles away from the trenches, but the fact that he was there, and that it was Smolenski who was giving the orders, was enough. Few had ever seen Smolenski, but his name was sufficient; it was as effective as is Mr. Bowen's name on a Bank of England note. It gave one a pleasant feeling to know that he was somewhere within call; you felt there would be no "routs" nor stampedes while he was there. And so for two days those seven thousand men lay in the trenches, repulsing attack after attack of the Turkish troops, suffocated with the heat and chilled with sudden showers, and swept unceasingly by shells and bullets - partly because they happened to be good men and brave men, but largely because they knew that somewhere behind them a stout, bull-necked soldier was sitting on a camp-stool, watching them through a pair of field-glasses.

Toward mid-day you would see a man leave the trench with a comrade's arm around him, and start on the long walk to the town where the hospital corps were waiting for him. These men did not wear their wounds with either pride or braggadocio, but regarded the wet sleeves and shapeless arms in a sort of wondering surprise. There was much more of surprise than of pain in their faces, and they seemed to be puzzling as to what they had done in the past to deserve such a punishment.

Other men were carried out of the trench and laid on their backs on the high grass, staring up drunkenly at the glaring sun, and with their limbs fallen into unfamiliar poses. They lay so still, and they were so utterly oblivious of the roar and rattle and the anxious energy around them that one grew rather afraid of them and of their superiority to their surroundings. The sun beat on them, and the insects in the grass waving above them buzzed and hummed, or burrowed in the warm moist earth upon which they lay; over their heads the invisible carriers of death jarred the air with shrill crescendoes, and near them a comrade sat hacking with his bayonet at a lump of hard bread. He sprawled contentedly in the hot sun, with humped shoulders and legs far apart, and with his cap tipped far over his eyes. Every now and again he would pause, with a piece of cheese balanced on the end of his knife-blade, and look at the twisted figures by him on the grass, or he would dodge involuntarily as a shell swung low above his head, and smile nervously at the still forms on either side of him that had not moved. Then he brushed the crumbs from his jacket and took a drink out of his hot canteen, and looking again at the sleeping figures pressing down the long grass beside him, crawled back on his hands and knees to the trench and picked up his waiting rifle.

The dead gave dignity to what the other men were doing, and made it noble, and, from another point of view, quite senseless. For their dying had proved nothing. Men who could have been much better spared than they, were still alive in the trenches, and for no reason but through mere dumb chance. There was no selection of the unfittest; it seemed to be ruled by unreasoning luck. A certain number of shells and bullets passed through a certain area of space, and men of different bulks blocked that space in different places. If a man happened to be standing in the line of a bullet he was killed and passed into eternity, leaving a wife and children, perhaps, to mourn him. "Father died," these children will say, "doing his duty." As a matter of fact, father died because he happened to stand up at the wrong moment, or because he turned to ask the man on his right for a match, instead of leaning toward the left, and he projected his bulk of two hundred pounds where a bullet, fired by a man who did not know him and who had not aimed at him, happened to want the right of way. One of the two had to give it, and as the bullet would not, the soldier had his heart torn out. The man who sat next to me happened to stoop to fill his cartridge-box just as the bullet that wanted the space he had occupied passed over his bent shoulder; and so he was not killed, but will live for sixty years, perhaps, and will do much good or much evil. Another man in the same trench sat up to clean his rifle, and had his arm in the air driving the cleaning rod down the barrel, when a bullet passed through his lungs, and the gun fell across his face, with the rod sticking in it, and he pitched forward on his shoulder quite dead. If he had not cleaned his gun at that moment he would probably be alive in Athens now, sitting in front of a cafe and fighting the war over again. Viewed from that point, and leaving out the fact that God ordered it all, the fortunes of the game of war seemed as capricious as matching pennies, and as impersonal as the wheel at Monte Carlo. In it the brave man did not win because he was brave, but because he was lucky. A fool and a philosopher are equal at a game of dice. And these men who threw dice with death were interesting to watch, because, though they gambled for so great a stake, they did so unconcernedly and without flinching, and without apparently appreciating the seriousness of the game.

There was a red-headed, freckled peasant boy, in dirty petticoats, who guided Bass and myself to the trenches. He was one of the few peasants who had not run away, and as he had driven sheep over every foot of the hills, he was able to guide the soldiers through those places where they were best protected from the bullets of the enemy. He did this all day, and was always, whether coming or going, under a heavy fire; but he enjoyed that fact, and he seemed to regard the battle only as a delightful change in the quiet routine of his life, as one of our own country boys at home would regard the coming of the spring circus or the burning of a neighbor's barn. He ran dancing ahead of us, pointing to where a ledge of rock offered a natural shelter, or showing us a steep gully where the bullets could not fall. When they came very near him he would jump high in the air, not because he was startled, but out of pure animal joy in the excitement of it, and he would frown importantly and shake his red curls at us, as though to say: "I told you to be careful. Now, you see. Don't let that happen again." We met him many times during the two days, escorting different companies of soldiers from one point to another, as though they were visitors to his estate. When a shell broke, he would pick up a piece and present it to the officer in charge, as though it were a flower he had plucked from his own garden, and which he wanted his guest to carry away with him as a souvenir of his visit. Some one asked the boy if his father and mother knew where he was, and he replied, with amusement, that they had run away and deserted him, and that he had remained because he wished to see what a Turkish army looked like. He was a much more plucky boy than the overrated Casabianca, who may have stood on the burning deck whence all but him had fled because he could not swim, and because it was with him a choice of being either burned or drowned. This boy stuck to the burning deck when it was possible for him at any time to have walked away and left it burning. But he stayed on because he was amused, and because he was able to help the soldiers from the city in safety across his native heath. He was much the best part of the show, and one of the bravest Greeks on the field. He will grow up to be something fine, no doubt, and his spirit will rebel against having to spend his life watching his father's sheep. He may even win the race from Marathon.

Another Greek who was a most interesting figure to us was a Lieutenant Ambroise Frantzis. He was in command of the mountain battery on the flat, round top of the high hill. On account of its height the place seemed much nearer to the sun than any other part of the world, and the heat there was three times as fierce as in the trenches below. When you had climbed to the top of this hill it was like standing on a roof-garden, or as though you were watching a naval battle from a fighting top of one of the battleships. The top of the hill was not unlike an immense circus ring in appearance. The piled-up earth around its circular edge gave that impression, and the glaring yellow wheat that was tramped into glaring yellow soil, and the blue ammunition-boxes scattered about, helped out the illusion. It was an exceedingly busy place, and the smoke drifted across it continually, hiding us from one another in a curtain of flying yellow dust, while over our heads the Turkish shells raced after each other so rapidly that they beat out the air like the branches of a tree in a storm. On account of its height, and the glaring heat, and the shells passing, and the Greek guns going off and then turning somersaults, it was not a place suited for meditation; but Ambroise Frantzis meditated there as though he were in his own study. He was a very young man and very shy, and he was too busy to consider his own safety, or to take time, as the others did, to show that he was not considering it.

Some of the other officers stood up on the breastworks and called the attention of the men to what they were doing; but as they did not wish the men to follow their example in this, it was difficult to see what they expected to gain by their braggadocio. Frantzis was as unconcerned as an artist painting a big picture in his studio. The battle plain below him was his canvas, and his nine mountain guns were his paint brushes. And he painted out Turks and Turkish cannon with the same concentrated, serious expression of countenance that you see on the face of an artist when he bites one brush between his lips and with another wipes out a false line or a touch of the wrong color. You have seen an artist cock his head on one side, and shut one eye and frown at his canvas, and then select several brushes and mix different colors and hit the canvas a bold stroke, and then lean back to note the effect. Frantzis acted in just that way. He would stand with his legs apart and his head on one side, pulling meditatively at his pointed beard, and then taking a closer look through his field-glasses, would select the three guns he had decided would give him the effect he wanted to produce, and he would produce that effect. When the shot struck plump in the Turkish lines, and we could see the earth leap up into the air like geysers of muddy water, and each gunner would wave his cap and cheer, Frantzis would only smile uncertainly, and begin again, with the aid of his field-glasses, to puzzle out fresh combinations.

The battle that had begun in a storm of hail ended on the first day in a storm of bullets that had been held in reserve by the Turks, and which let off just after sundown. They came from a natural trench, formed by the dried-up bed of a stream which lay just below the hill on which the first Greek trench was situated. There were bushes growing on the bank of the stream nearest to the Greek lines, and these hid the men who occupied it. Throughout the day there had been an irritating fire from this trench from what appeared to be not more than a dozen rifles, but we could see that it was fed from time to time with many boxes of ammunition, which were carried to it on the backs of mules from the Turkish position a half mile farther to the rear. Bass and a corporal took a great aversion to this little group of Turks, not because there were too many of them to be disregarded, but because they were so near; and Bass kept the corporal's services engaged in firing into it, and in discouraging the ammunition mules when they were being driven in that direction. Our corporal was a sharp-shooter, and, accordingly, felt his superiority to his comrades; and he had that cheerful contempt for his officers that all true Greek soldiers enjoy; and so he never joined in the volley-firing, but kept his ammunition exclusively for the dozen men behind the bushes and for the mules. He waged, as it were, a little battle on his own account. The other men rose as commanded and fired regular volleys, and sank back again, but he fixed his sights to suit his own idea of the range, and he rose when he was ready to do so, and fired whenever he thought best. When his officer, who kept curled up in the hollow of the trench, commanded him to lie down, he would frown and shake his head at the interruption, and paid no further attention to the order. He was as much alone as a hunter on a mountain peak stalking deer, and whenever he fired at the men in the bushes he would swear softly, and when he fired at the mules he would chuckle and laugh with delight and content. The mules had to cross a ploughed field in order to reach the bushes, and so we were able to mark where his bullets struck, and we could see them skip across the field, kicking up the dirt as they advanced, until they stopped the mule altogether, or frightened the man who was leading it into a disorderly retreat.

It appeared later that instead of there being but twelve men in these bushes there were six hundred, and that they were hiding there until the sun set in order to make a final attack on the first trench. They had probably argued that at sunset the strain of the day's work would have told on the Greek morale, that the men's nerves would be jerking and their stomachs aching for food, and that they would be ready for darkness and sleep, and in no condition to repulse a fresh and vigorous attack. So, just as the sun sank, and the officers were counting the cost in dead and wounded, and the men were gathering up blankets and overcoats, and the firing from the Greek lines had almost ceased, there came a fierce rattle from the trench to the right of us, like a watch-dog barking the alarm, and the others took it up from all over the hill, and when we looked down into the plain below to learn what it meant, we saw it blue with men, who seemed to have sprung from the earth. They were clambering from the bed of the stream, breaking through the bushes, and forming into a long line, which, as soon as formed, was at once hidden at regular intervals by flashes of flame that seemed to leap from one gun-barrel to the next, as you have seen a current of electricity run along a line of gas-jets. In the dim twilight these flashes were much more blinding than they had been in the glare of the sun, and the crash of the artillery coming on top of the silence was the more fierce and terrible by the contrast. The Turks were so close on us that the first trench could do little to help itself, and the men huddled against it while their comrades on the surrounding hills fought for them, their volleys passing close above our heads, and meeting the rush of the Turkish bullets on the way, so that there was now one continuous whistling shriek, like the roar of the wind through the rigging of a ship in a storm. If a man had raised his arm above his head his hand would have been torn off. It had come up so suddenly that it was like two dogs, each springing at the throat of the other, and in a greater degree it had something of the sound of two wild animals struggling for life. Volley answered volley as though with personal hate - one crashing in upon the roll of the other, or beating it out of recognition with the bursting roar of heavy cannon. At the same instant all of the Turkish batteries opened with great, ponderous, booming explosions, and the little mountain guns barked and snarled and shrieked back at them, and the rifle volleys crackled and shot out blistering flames, while the air was filled with invisible express trains that shook and jarred it and crashed into one another, bursting and shrieking and groaning. It seemed as though you were lying in a burning forest, with giant tree trunks that had withstood the storms of centuries crashing and falling around your ears, and sending up great showers of sparks and flame. This lasted for five minutes or less, and then the death-grip seemed to relax, the volleys came brokenly, like a man panting for breath, the bullets ceased to sound with the hiss of escaping steam, and rustled aimlessly by, and from hill-top to hill-top the officers' whistles sounded as though a sportsman were calling off his dogs. The Turks withdrew into the coming night, and the Greeks lay back, panting and sweating, and stared open-eyed at one another, like men who had looked for a moment into hell, and had come back to the world again.

The next day was like the first, except that by five

o'clock in the afternoon the Turks appeared on our left flank, crawling across the hills like an invasion of great ants, and the Greek army that at Velestinos had made the two best and most dignified stands of the war withdrew upon Halmyros, and the Turks poured into the village and burned it, leaving nothing standing save two tall Turkish minarets that many years before, when Thessaly belonged to the Sultan, the Turks themselves had placed there.

THE SPANISH-AMERICAN WAR

I - THE ROUGH RIDERS AT GUASIMAS

On the day the American troops landed on the coast of Cuba, the Cubans informed General Wheeler that the enemy were intrenched at Guasimas, blocking the way to Santiago. Guasimas is not a village, nor even a collection of houses; it is the meeting place of two trails which join at the apex of a V, three miles from the seaport town of Siboney, and continue merged in a single trail to Santiago. General Wheeler, guided by the Cubans, reconnoitred this trail on the 23rd of June, and with the position of the enemy fully explained to him, returned to Siboney and informed General Young and Colonel Wood that on the following morning he would attack the Spanish position at Guasimas. It has been stated that at Guasimas, the Rough Riders were trapped in an ambush, but, as the plan was discussed while I was present, I know that so far from any ones running into an ambush, every one of the officers concerned had a full knowledge of where he would find the enemy, and what he was to do when he found him.

That night no one slept, for until two o'clock in the morning, troops were still being disembarked in the surf, and two ships of war had their searchlights turned on the landing-place, and made Siboney as light as a ball-room. Back of the searchlights was an ocean white with moonlight, and on the shore red camp-fires, at which the half-drowned troops were drying their uniforms, and the Rough Riders, who had just marched in from Baiquiri, were cooking a late supper, or early breakfast of coffee and bacon. Below the former home of the Spanish comandante, which General Wheeler had made his head-quarters, lay the camp of the Rough Riders, and through it Cuban officers were riding their half-starved ponies, and scattering the ashes of the camp-fires. Below them was the beach and the roaring surf, in which a thousand or so naked men were assisting and impeding the progress shoreward of their comrades, in pontoons and shore boats, which were being hurled at the beach like sleds down a water chute.

It was one of the most weird and remarkable scenes of the war, probably of any war. An army was being landed on an enemy's coast at the dead of night, but with the same cheers and shrieks and laughter that rise from the bathers at Coney Island on a hot Sunday. It was a pandemonium of noises. The men still to be landed from the "prison hulks," as they called the transports, were singing in chorus, the men already on shore were dancing naked around the camp-fires on the beach, or shouting with delight as they plunged into the first bath that had offered in seven days, and those in the launches as they were pitched head-first at the soil of Cuba, signalized their arrival by howls of triumph. On either side rose black overhanging ridges, in the lowland between were white tents and burning fires, and from the ocean came the blazing, dazzling eyes of the search-lights shaming the quiet moonlight.

After three hours' troubled sleep in this tumult the

Rough Riders left camp at five in the morning. With the exception of half a dozen officers they were dismounted, and carried their blanket rolls, haversacks, ammunition, and carbines. General Young had already started toward Guasimas the First and Tenth dismounted Cavalry, and according to the agreement of the night before had taken the eastern trail to our right, while the Rough Riders climbed the steep ridge above Siboney and started toward the rendezvous along the trail to the west, which was on high ground and a half mile to a mile distant from the trail along which General Young and his regulars were marching. There was a valley between us, and the bushes were so thick on both sides of our trail that it was not possible at any time, until we met at Guasimas, to distinguish the other column.

As soon as the Rough Riders had reached the top of the ridge, not twenty minutes after they had left camp, which was the first opportunity that presented itself, Colonel Wood ordered Captain Capron to proceed with his troop in front of the column as an advance guard, and to choose a "point" of five men skilled as scouts and trailers. Still in advance of these he placed two Cuban scouts. The column then continued along the trail in single file. The Cubans were at a distance of two hundred and fifty yards; the "point" of five picked men under Sergeant Byrne and duty-Sergeant Fish followed them at a distance of a hundred yards, and then came Capron's troop of sixty men strung out in single file. No flankers were placed for the reason that the dense undergrowth and the tangle of vines that stretched from the branches of the trees to the bushes below made it a physical impossibility for man or beast to move forward except along the single trail.

Colonel Wood rode at the head of the column, followed by two regular army officers who were members of General Wheeler's staff, a Cuban officer, and Lieutenant-Colonel Roosevelt. They rode slowly in consideration of the troopers on foot, who under a cruelly hot sun carried heavy burdens. To those who did not have to walk, it was not unlike a hunting excursion in our West; the scenery was beautiful and the view down the valley one of luxuriant peace. Roosevelt had never been in the tropics and Captain McCormick and I were talking back at him over our shoulders and at each other, pointing out unfamiliar trees and birds. Roosevelt thought it looked like a good deer country, as it once was; it reminded McCormick of Southern California; it looked to me like the trails in Central America. We advanced, talking in that fashion and in high spirits, and congratulating ourselves in being shut of the transport and on breathing fine mountain air again, and on the fact that we were on horseback. We agreed it was impossible to appreciate that we were really at war - that we were in the enemy's country. We had been riding in this pleasant fashion for an hour and a half with brief halts for rest, when Wood stopped the head of the column, and rode down the trail to meet Capron, who was coming back. Wood returned immediately, leading his horse, and said to Roosevelt:

"Pass the word back to keep silence in the ranks."

The place at which we had halted was where the trail narrowed, and proceeded sharply downward. There was on one side of it a stout barbed-wire fence of five strands. By some fortunate accident this fence had been cut just where the head of the column halted. On the left of the trail it shut off fields of high grass blocked at every fifty yards with great barricades of undergrowth and tangled trees and chapparal. On the other side of the trail there was not a foot of free ground; the bushes seemed absolutely impenetrable, as indeed they were later found to be.

When we halted, the men sat down beside the trail and chewed the long blades of grass, or fanned the air with their hats. They had no knowledge of the situation such as their leaders possessed, and their only emotion was one of satisfaction at the chance the halt gave them to rest and to shift their packs. Wood again walked down the trail with Capron and disappeared, and one of the officers informed us that the scouts had seen the outposts of the enemy. It did not seem reasonable that the Spaniards, who had failed to attack us when we landed at Baiquiri, would oppose us until they could do so in force, so, personally, I doubted that there were any Spaniards nearer than Santiago. But we tied our horses to the wire fence, and Capron's troop knelt with carbines at the "Ready," peering into the bushes. We must have waited there, while Wood reconnoitred, for over ten minutes. Then he returned, and began deploying his troops out at either side of the trail. Capron he sent on down the trail itself. G Troop was ordered to beat into the bushes on the right, and K and A were sent over the ridge on which we stood down into the hollow to connect with General Young's column on the opposite side of the valley. F and E Troops were deployed in skirmish-line on the other side of the wire fence. Wood had discovered the enemy a few hundred yards from where he expected to find him, and so far from being "surprised," he had time, as I have just described, to get five of his troops into position before a shot was fired. The firing, when it came, started suddenly on our right. It sounded so close that - still believing we were acting on a false alarm, and that there were no Spaniards ahead of us - I guessed it was Capron's men firing at random to disclose the enemy's position. I ran after G Troop under Captain Llewellyn, and found them breaking their way through the bushes in the direction from which the volleys came. It was like forcing the walls of a maze. If each trooper had not kept in touch with the man on either hand he would have been lost in the thicket. At one moment the underbrush seemed swarming with our men, and the next, except that you heard the twigs breaking, and heavy breathing or a crash as a vine pulled some one down, there was not a sign of a human being anywhere. In a few minutes we broke through into a little open place in front of a dark curtain of vines, and the men fell on one knee and began returning the fire that came from it.

The enemy's fire was exceedingly heavy, and his aim was excellent. We saw nothing of the Spaniards, except a few on the ridge across the valley. I happened to be the only one present with field glasses, and when I discovered this force on the ridge, and had made sure, by the cockades in their sombreros, that they were Spaniards and not Cubans, I showed them to Roosevelt. He calculated they were five hundred yards from us, and ordered the men to fire on them at that range. Through the two hours of fighting that followed, although men were falling all around us, the Spaniards on the ridge were the only ones that many of us saw. But the fire against us was not more than eighty yards away, and so hot that our men could only lie flat in the grass and return it in that position. It was at this moment that our men believed they were being attacked by Capron's troop, which they imagined must have swung to the right, and having lost its bearings and hearing them advancing through the underbrush, had mistaken them for the enemy. They accordingly ceased firing and began shouting in order to warn Capron that he was shooting at his friends. This is the foundation for the statement that the Rough Riders had fired on each other, which they did not do then or at any other time. Later we examined the relative position of the trail which Capron held, and the position of G Troop, and they were at right angles to one another.

Capron could not possibly have fired into us at any time, unless he had turned directly around in his tracks and aimed up the very trail he had just descended. Advancing, he could no more have hit us than he could have seen us out of the back of his head. When we found many hundred spent cartridges of the Spaniards a hundred yards in front of G Troop's position, the question as to who had fired on us was answered.

It was an exceedingly hot corner. The whole troop was gathered in the little open place blocked by the network of grape-vines and tangled bushes before it. They could not see twenty feet on three sides of them, but on the right hand lay the valley, and across it came the sound of Young's brigade, who were apparently heavily engaged. The enemy's fire was so close that the men could not hear the word of command, and Captain Llewellyn and Lieutenant Greenway, unable to get their attention, ran among them, batting them with their sombreros to make them cease firing. Lieutenant-Colonel Roosevelt ran up just then, bringing with him Lieutenant Woodbury Kane and ten troopers from K Troop. Roosevelt lay down in the grass beside Llewellyn and consulted with him eagerly. Kane was smiling with the charming content of a perfectly happy man. When Captain Llewellyn told him his men were not needed, and to rejoin his troop, he led his detail over the edge of the hill on which we lay. As he disappeared below the crest he did not stoop to avoid the bullets, but walked erect, still smiling. Roosevelt pointed out that it was impossible to advance farther on account of the network of wild grape-vines that masked the Spaniards from us, and that we must cross the trail and make to the left. The shouts the men had raised to warn Capron had established our position to the enemy, and the firing was now fearfully accurate. Sergeant Russell, who in his day had been a colonel on a governor's staff, was killed, and the other sergeant was shot through the wrist. In the space of three minutes nine men were lying on their backs helpless. Before we got away, every third man was killed, or wounded. We drew off slowly to the left, dragging the wounded with us. Owing to the low aim of the enemy, we were forced to move on our knees and crawl. Even then men were hit. One man near me was shot through the head. Returning later to locate the body and identify him, I found that the buzzards had torn off his lips and his eyes. This mutilation by these hideous birds was, without doubt, what Admiral Sampson mistook for the work of the Spaniards, when the bodies of the marines at Guantanamo were found disfigured. K Troop meantime had deployed into the valley under the fire from the enemy on the ridge. It had been ordered to establish communication with General Young's column, and while advancing and firing on the ridge, Captain Jenkins sent the guidon bearer back to climb the hill and wave his red and white banner where Young's men could see it. The guidon bearer had once run for Congress on the gold ticket in Arizona, and, as some one said, was naturally the man who should have been selected for a forlorn hope. His flag brought him instantly under a heavy fire, but he continued waving it until the Tenth Cavalry on the other side of the valley answered, and the two columns were connected by a skirmish-line composed of K Troop and A, under Captain "Bucky" O'Neill.

G Troop meanwhile had hurried over to the left, and passing through the opening in the wire fence had spread out into open order. It followed down after Captain Luna's troop and D and E Troops, which were well already in advance. Roosevelt ran forward and took command of the extreme left of this line. Wood was walking up and down along it, leading his horse, which he thought might be of use in case he had to move quickly to alter his original formation. His plan, at present, was to spread out his men so that they would join Young on the right, and on the left swing around until they flanked the enemy. K and A Troops had already succeeded in joining hands with Young's column across the valley, and as they were capable of taking care of themselves, Wood was bending his efforts to keep his remaining four companies in a straight line and revolving them around the enemy's "end." It was in no way an easy thing to do. The men were at times wholly hidden from each other, and from him; probably at no one time did he see more than two of his troops together. It was only by the firing that he could tell where his men lay, and that they were always advancing.

The advances were made in quick, desperate rushes - sometimes the ground gained was no more than a man covers in sliding for a base. At other times half a troop would rise and race forward and then burrow deep in the hot grass and fire. On this side of the line there was an occasional glimpse of the enemy. But for a great part of the time the men shot at the places from where the enemy's fire seemed to come, aiming low and answering in steady volleys. The fire discipline was excellent. The prophets of evil of the Tampa Bay Hotel had foretold that the cowboys would shoot as they chose, and, in the field, would act independently of their officers. As it turned out, the cowboys were the very men who waited most patiently for the officers to give the word of command. At all times the movement was without rest, breathless and fierce, like a cane-rush, or a street fight. After the first three minutes every man had stripped as though for a wrestling match, throwing off all his impedimenta but his cartridge-belt and canteen. Even then the sun handicapped their strength cruelly. The enemy was hidden in the shade of the jungle, while they, for every thicket they gained, had to fight in the open, crawling through grass which was as hot as a steam bath, and with their flesh and clothing torn by thorns and the sword-like blade of the Spanish "bayonet." The glare of the sun was full in their eyes and as fierce as a lime-light.

When G Troop passed on across the trail to the left I stopped at the place where the column had first halted - it had been converted into a dressing station and the wounded of G Troop were left there in the care of the hospital stewards. A tall, gaunt young man with a cross on his arm was just coming back up the trail. His head was bent, and by some surgeon's trick he was carrying a wounded man much heavier than himself across his shoulders. As I stepped out of the trail he raised his head, and smiled and nodded, and left me wondering where I had seen him before, smiling in the same cheery, confident way and moving in that same position. I knew it could not have been under the same conditions, and yet he was certainly associated with another time of excitement and rush and heat. Then I remembered him. As now he had been covered with blood and dirt and perspiration, but then he wore a canvas jacket and the man he carried on his shoulders was trying to hold him back from a white-washed line. And I recognized the young doctor, with the blood bathing his breeches, as "Bob" Church, of Princeton. That was only one of four badly wounded men he carried that day on his shoulders over a half-mile of trail that stretched from the firing-line back to the dressing station and under an unceasing fire. {3} As the senior surgeon was absent he had chief responsibility that day for all the wounded, and that so few of them died is greatly due to this young man who went down into the firing-line and pulled them from it, and bore them out of danger. The comic paragraphers who wrote of the members of the Knickerbocker Club and the college swells of the Rough Riders and of their imaginary valets and golf clubs, should, in decency, since the fight at Guasimas apologize. For the same spirit that once sent these men down a white-washed field against their opponents' rush line was the spirit that sent Church, Channing, Devereux, Ronalds, Wrenn, Cash, Bull, Lamed, Goodrich, Greenway, Dudley Dean, and a dozen others through the high hot grass at Guasimas, not shouting, as their friends the cowboys did, but each with his mouth tightly shut, with his eyes on the ball, and moving in obedience to the captain's signals.

Judging from the sound, our firing-line now seemed to be half a mile in advance of the place where the head of the column had first halted. This showed that the Spaniards had been driven back at least three hundred yards from their original position. It was impossible to see any of our men in the field, so I ran down the trail with the idea that it would lead me back to the troop I had left when I had stopped at the dressing station. The walk down that trail presented one of the most grewsome pictures of the war. It narrowed as it descended; it was for that reason the enemy had selected that part of it for the attack, and the vines and bushes interlaced so closely above it that the sun could not come through.

The rocks on either side were spattered with blood and the rank grass was matted with it. Blanket rolls, haversacks, carbines, and canteens had been abandoned all along its length. It looked as though a retreating army had fled along it, rather than that one troop had fought its way through it to the front. Except for the clatter of the land-crabs, those hideous orchid-colored monsters that haunt the places of the dead, and the whistling of the bullets in the trees, the place was as silent as a grave. For the wounded lying along its length were as still as the dead beside them. The noise of the loose stones rolling under my feet brought a hospital steward out of the brush, and he called after me:

"Lieutenant Thomas is badly wounded in here, and we can't move him. We want to carry him out of the sun some place, where there is shade and a breeze." Thomas was the first lieutenant of Capron's troop. He is a young man, large and powerfully built. He was shot through the leg just below the trunk, and I found him lying on a blanket half naked and covered with blood, and with his leg bound in tourniquets made of twigs and pocket-handkerchiefs. It gave one a thrill of awe and wonder to see how these cowboy surgeons, with a stick that one would use to light a pipe and with the gaudy 'kerchiefs they had taken from their necks, were holding death at bay. The young officer was in great pain and tossing and raving wildly. When we gathered up the corners of his blanket and lifted him, he tried to sit upright, and cried out, "You're taking me to the front, aren't you? You said you would. They've killed my captain - do you understand? They've killed Captain Capron. The - Mexicans! They've killed my captain."

The troopers assured him they were carrying him to the firing-line, but he was not satisfied. We stumbled over the stones and vines, bumping his wounded body against the ground and leaving a black streak in the grass behind us, but it seemed to hurt us more than it did him, for he sat up again clutching at us imploringly with his bloody hands.

"For God's sake, take me to the front," he begged. "Do you hear? I order you; damn you, I order - We must give them hell; do you hear? we must give them hell. They've killed Capron. They've killed my captain."

The loss of blood at last mercifully silenced him, and when we had reached the trail he had fainted and I left them kneeling around him, their grave boyish faces filled with sympathy and concern.

Only fifty feet from him and farther down the trail I passed his captain, with his body propped against Church's knee and with his head fallen on the surgeon's shoulder. Capron was always a handsome, soldierly looking man - some said that he was the most soldierly looking of any of the young officers in the army - and as I saw him then death had given him a great dignity and nobleness. He was only twenty-eight years old, the age when life has just begun, but he rested his head on the surgeon's shoulder like a man who knew he was already through with it and that, though they might peck and mend at the body, he had received his final orders. His breast and shoulders were bare, and as the surgeon cut the tunic from him the sight of his great chest and the skin, as white as a girl's, and the black open wound against it made the yellow stripes and the brass insignia on the tunic, strangely mean and tawdry.

Fifty yards farther on, around a turn in the trail, behind a rock, a boy was lying with a bullet wound between his eyes. His chest was heaving with short, hoarse noises which I guessed were due to some muscular action entirely, and that he was virtually dead. I lifted him and gave him some water, but it would not pass through his fixed teeth. In the pocket of his blouse was a New Testament with the name Fielder Dawson, Mo., scribbled in it in pencil. While I was writing it down for identification, a boy as young as himself came from behind me down the trail.

"It is no use," he said; "the surgeon has seen him; he says he is just the same as dead. He is my bunkie; we only met two weeks ago at San Antonio; but he and me had got to be such good friends - But there's nothing I can do now." He threw himself down on the rock beside his bunkie, who was still breathing with that hoarse inhuman rattle, and I left them, the one who had been spared looking down helplessly with the tears creeping across his cheeks.

The firing was quite close now, and the trail was no longer filled with blanket rolls and haversacks, nor did pitiful, prostrate figures lie in wait behind each rock. I guessed this must mean that I now was well in advance of the farthest point to which Capron's troop had moved, and I was running forward feeling confident that I must be close on our men, when I saw the body of a sergeant blocking the trail and stretched at full length across it. Its position was a hundred yards in advance of that of any of the others - it was apparently the body of the first man killed. After death the bodies of some men seem to shrink almost instantly within themselves; they become limp and shapeless, and their uniforms hang upon them strangely. But this man, who was a giant in life, remained a giant in death - his very attitude was one of attack; his fists were clinched, his jaw set, and his eyes, which were still human, seemed fixed with resolve. He was dead, but he was not defeated. And so Hamilton Fish died as he had lived - defiantly, running into the very face of the enemy, standing squarely upright on his legs instead of crouching, as the others called to him to do, until he fell like a column across the trail. "God gives," was the motto on the watch I took from his blouse, and God could not have given him a nobler end; to die, in the fore-front of the first fight of the war, quickly, painlessly, with a bullet through the heart, with his regiment behind him, and facing the enemies of his country.

The line at this time was divided by the trail into two wings. The right wing, composed of K and A Troops, was advancing through the valley, returning the fire from the ridge as it did so, and the left wing, which was much the longer of the two, was swinging around on the enemy's right flank, with its own right resting on the barbed-wire fence. I borrowed a carbine from a wounded man, and joined the remnant of L Troop which was close to the trail.

This troop was then commanded by Second Lieutenant

Day, who on account of his conduct that morning and at the battle of San Juan later, when he was shot through the arm, was promoted to be captain of L Troop, or, as it was later officially designated, Capron's troop. He was walking up and down the line as unconcernedly as though we were at target practice, and an Irish sergeant, Byrne, was assisting him by keeping up a continuous flow of comments and criticisms that showed the keenest enjoyment of the situation. Byrne was the only man I noticed who seemed to regard the fight as in any way humorous. For at Guasimas, no one had time to be flippant, or to exhibit any signs of braggadocio. It was for all of them, from the moment it started, through the hot, exhausting hour and a half that it lasted, a most serious proposition. The conditions were exceptional. The men had made a night march the evening before, had been given but three hours' troubled sleep on the wet sand, and had then been marched in full equipment uphill and under a cruelly hot sun, directly into action. And eighty per cent. of them had never before been under fire. Nor had one man in the regiment ever fired a Krag-Jorgensen carbine until he fired it at a Spaniard, for their arms had been issued to them so soon before sailing that they had only drilled with them without using cartridges. To this handicap was also added the nature of the ground and the fact that our men could not see their opponents. Their own men fell or rolled over on every side, shot down by an invisible enemy, with no one upon whom they could retaliate, with no sign that the attack might not go on indefinitely. Yet they never once took a step backward, but advanced grimly, cleaning a bush or thicket of its occupants before charging it, and securing its cover for themselves, and answering each volley with one that sounded like an echo of the first. The men were panting for breath; the sweat ran so readily into their eyes that they could not see the sights of their guns; their limbs unused to such exertion after seven days of cramped idleness on the troop-ship, trembled with weakness and the sun blinded and dazzled them; but time after time they rose and staggered forward through the high grass, or beat their way with their carbines against the tangle of vines and creepers. A mile and a half of territory was gained foot by foot in this fashion, the three Spanish positions carried in that distance being marked by the thousands of Mauser cartridges that lay shining and glittering in the grass and behind the barricades of bushes. But this distance had not been gained without many losses, for every one in the regiment was engaged. Even those who, on account of the heat, had dropped out along the trail, as soon as the sound of the fight reached them, came limping to the front - and plunged into the firing-line. It was the only place they could go - there was no other line. With the exception of Church's dressing station and its wounded there were no reserves.

Among the first to be wounded was the correspondent, Edward Marshall, of the New York Journal, who was on the firing-line to the left. He was shot through the body near the spine, and when I saw him he was suffering the most terrible agonies, and passing through a succession of convulsions. He nevertheless, in his brief moments of comparative peace, bore himself with the utmost calm, and was so much a soldier to duty that he continued writing his account of the fight until the fight itself was ended. His courage was the admiration of all the troopers, and he was highly commended by Colonel Wood in the official account of the engagement.

Nothing so well illustrated how desperately each man was needed, and how little was his desire to withdraw, as the fact that the wounded lay where they fell until the hospital stewards found them. Their comrades did not use them as an excuse to go to leave the firing-line. I have watched other fights, where the men engaged were quite willing to unselfishly bear the wounded from the zone of danger.

The fight had now lasted an hour, and the line had reached a more open country, with a slight incline upward toward a wood, on the edge of which was a ruined house. This house was a former distillery for aguardiente, and was now occupied in force by the enemy. Lieutenant-Colonel Roosevelt on the far left was moving up his men with the intention of taking this house on the flank; Wood, who was all over the line, had the same objective point in his mind. The troop commanders had a general idea that the distillery was the key to the enemy's position, and were all working in that direction. It was extremely difficult for Wood and Roosevelt to communicate with the captains, and after the first general orders had been given them they relied upon the latter's intelligence to pull them through. I do not suppose Wood, out of the five hundred engaged, saw more than thirty of his men at any one time. When he had passed one troop, except for the noise of its volley firing, it was immediately lost to him in the brush, and it was so with the next. Still, so excellent was the intelligence of the officers, and so ready the spirit of the men, that they kept an almost perfect alignment, as was shown when the final order came to charge in the open fields. The advance upon the ruined building was made in stubborn, short rushes, sometimes in silence, and sometimes firing as we ran. The order to fire at will was seldom given, the men waiting patiently for the officers' signal, and then answering in volleys. Some of the men who were twice Day's age begged him to let them take the enemy's impromptu fort on the run, but he answered them tolerantly like spoiled children, and held them down until there was a lull in the enemy's fire, when he would lead them forward, always taking the advance himself. By the way they made these rushes, it was easy to tell which men were used to hunting big game in the West and which were not. The Eastern men broke at the word, and ran for the cover they were directed to take like men trying to get out of the rain, and fell panting on their faces, while the Western trappers and hunters slipped and wriggled through the grass like Indians; dodging from tree trunk to tree trunk, and from one bush to another. They fell into line at the same time with the others, but while doing so they had not once exposed themselves. Some of the escapes were little short of miraculous. The man on my right, Champneys Marshall, of Washington, had one bullet pass through his sleeve, and another pass through his shirt, where it was pulled close to his spine. The holes where the ball entered and went out again were clearly cut. Another man's skin was slightly burned by three bullets in three distinct lines, as though it had been touched for an instant by the lighted end of a cigar. Greenway was shot through this shirt across the breast, and Roosevelt was so close to one bullet, when it struck a tree, that it filled his eyes and ears with tiny splinters. Major Brodie and Lieutenant Thomas were both wounded within a few feet of Colonel Wood, and his color-sergeant, Wright, who followed close at his heels, was clipped three times in the head and neck, and four bullets passed through the folds of the flag he carried. One trooper, Rowland, of Deming, was shot through the lower ribs; he was ordered by Roosevelt to fall back to the dressing station, but there Church told him there was nothing he could do for him then, and directed him to sit down until he could be taken to the hospital at Siboney. Rowland sat still for a short time, and then remarked restlessly, "I don't seem to be doing much good here," and picking up his carbine, returned to the firing-line. There Roosevelt found him.

"I thought I ordered you to the rear," he demanded.

"Yes, sir, you did," Rowland said, "but there didn't seem to be much doing back there."

After the fight he was sent to Siboney with the rest of the wounded, but two days later he appeared in camp. He had marched from Siboney, a distance of six miles, and uphill all the way, carrying his carbine, canteen, and cartridge-belt.

"I thought you were in hospital," Wood said. "I was," Rowland answered sheepishly, "but I didn't seem to be doing any good there."

They gave him up as hopeless, and he continued his duties and went into the fight of the San Juan hills with the hole still through his ribs. Another cowboy named Heffner, when shot through the body, asked to be propped up against a tree with his canteen and cartridge-belt beside him, and the last his troop saw of him he was seated alone grimly firing over their heads in the direction of the enemy.

Early in the fight I came upon Church attending to a young cowboy, who was shot through the chest. The entrance to his wound was so small that Church could not insert enough of the gauze packing to stop the flow of blood.

"I'm afraid I'll have to make this hole larger, he said to the boy, "or you'll bleed to death."

"All right," the trooper answered, "I guess you know your business." The boy stretched out on his back and lay perfectly quiet while Church, with a pair of curved scissors, cut away the edges of the wound. His patient neither whimpered nor swore, but stared up at the sun in silence. The bullets were falling on every side, and the operation was a hasty one, but the trooper made no comment until Church said, "We'd better get out of this; can you stand being carried?"

"Do you think you can carry me?" the trooper asked.

"Yes."

"Well," exclaimed the boy admiringly, "you certainly know your business!"

Another of the Rough Riders was brought to the dressing station with a shattered ankle, and Church, after bandaging it, gave him his choice of riding down to Siboney on a mule, or of being carried, a day later, on a litter.

"If you think you can manage to ride the mule with that broken foot," he said, "you can start at once, but if you wait until to-morrow, when I can spare the men, you can be carried all the way."

The cowboy preferred to start at once, so six hospital stewards lifted him and dropped him on the mule, and into a huge Mexican saddle.

He stuck his wounded ankle into one stirrup, and his untouched one into the other, and gathered up the reins.

"Does it pain you? Can you stand it?" Church asked anxiously. The cowboy turned and smiled down upon him with amused disdain.

"Stand THIS?" he cried. "Why, this is just like getting money from home."

Toward the last, the firing from the enemy sounded less near, and the bullets passed much higher. Roosevelt, who had picked up a carbine and was firing to give the direction to the others, determined upon a charge. Wood, at the other end of the line, decided at the same time upon the same manoeuvre. It was called "Wood's bluff" afterward, for he had nothing to back it with; while to the enemy it looked as though his whole force was but the skirmish-line in advance of a regiment. The Spaniards naturally could not believe that this thin line which suddenly broke out of the bushes and from behind trees and came cheering out into the hot sunlight was the entire fighting force against it. They supposed the regiment was coming close on its heels, and as Spanish troops hate being rushed as a cat hates water, they fired a few parting volleys and broke and ran. The cheering had the same invigorating effect on our own side as a cold shower; it was what first told half the men where the other half were, and it made every individual man feel better. As we knew it was only a bluff, the first cheer was wavering, but the sound of our own voices was so comforting that the second cheer was a howl of triumph.

As it was, the Spaniards thought the Rough Riders had already disregarded all the rules of war.

"When we fired a volley," one of the prisoners said later, "instead of falling back they came forward. That is not the way to fight, to come closer at every volley." And so, when instead of retreating on each volley, the Rough Riders rushed at them, cheering and filling the hot air with wild cowboy yells, the dismayed enemy retreated upon Santiago, where he announced he had been attacked by the entire American army.

One of the residents of Santiago asked one of the soldiers if those Americans fought well.

"WELL!" he replied, "they tried to catch us with their hands!"

I have not attempted to give any account of General Young's fight on our right, which was equally desperate, and, owing to the courage of the colored troops of the Tenth in storming a ridge, equally worthy of praise. But it has seemed better not to try and tell of anything I did not see, but to limit myself to the work of the Rough Riders, to whom, after all, the victory was due, as it was owing to Colonel Wood's charge, which took the Spaniards in flank, that General Wheeler and General Young were able to advance, their own stubborn attack in front having failed to dislodge the enemy from his rifle-pits.

According to the statement of the enemy, who had every reason not to exaggerate the size of his own force, 4,000 Spaniards were engaged in this action.

The Rough Riders numbered 534, and General Young's force numbered 464. The American troops accordingly attacked a force over four times their own number intrenched behind rifle-pits and bushes in a mountain pass. In spite of the smokeless powder used by the Spaniards, which hid their position, the Rough Riders routed them out of it, and drove them back from three different barricades until they made their last stand in the ruined distillery, whence they finally drove them by assault. The eager spirit in which this was accomplished is best described in the Spanish soldier's answer to the inquiring civilian, "They tried to catch us with their hands." The Rough Riders should adopt it as their motto.

II - THE BATTLE OF SAN JUAN HILL

After the Guasimas fight on June 24, the army was advanced along the single trail which leads from Siboney on the coast to Santiago. Two streams of excellent water run parallel with this trail for short distances, and some eight miles from the coast crossed it in two places. Our outposts were stationed at the first of these fords, the Cuban outposts a mile and a half farther on at the ford nearer Santiago, where the stream made a sharp turn at a place called El Poso. Another mile and a half of trail extended from El Poso to the trenches of San Juan. The reader should remember El Poso, as it marked an important starting-point against San Juan on the eventful first of July.

For six days the army was encamped on either side of the trail for three miles back from the outposts. The regimental camps touched each other, and all day long the pack-trains carrying the day's rations passed up and down between them. The trail was a sunken wagon road, where it was possible, in a few places, for two wagons to pass at one time, but the greater distances were so narrow that there was but just room for a wagon, or a loaded mule-train, to make its way. The banks of the trail were three or four feet high, and when it rained it was converted into a huge gutter, with sides of mud, and with a liquid mud a foot deep between them. The camps were pitched along the trail as near the parallel stream as possible, and in the occasional places where there was rich, high grass. At night the men slept in dog tents, open at the front and back, and during the day spent their time under the shade of trees along the trail, or on the banks of the stream. Sentries were placed at every few feet along these streams to guard them from any possible pollution. For six days the army rested in this way, for as an army moves and acts only on its belly, and as the belly of this army was three miles long, it could advance but slowly.

This week of rest, after the cramped life of the troopship, was not ungrateful, although the rations were scarce and there was no tobacco, which was as necessary to the health of the men as their food.

During this week of waiting, the chief excitement was to walk out a mile and a half beyond the outposts to the hill of El Poso, and look across the basin that lay in the great valley which leads to Santiago. The left of the valley was the hills which hide the sea. The right of the valley was the hills in which nestle the village of El Caney. Below El Poso, in the basin, the dense green forest stretched a mile and a half to the hills of San Juan. These hills looked so quiet and sunny and well kept that they reminded one of a New England orchard. There was a blue bungalow on a hill to the right, a red bungalow higher up on the right, and in the centre the block-house of San Juan, which looked like a Chinese pagoda. Three-quarters of a mile behind them, with a dip between, were the long white walls of the hospital and barracks of Santiago, wearing thirteen Red Cross flags, and, as was pointed out to the foreign attaches later, two six-inch guns a hundred yards in advance of the Red Cross flags.

It was so quiet, so fair, and so prosperous looking that it breathed of peace. It seemed as though one might, without accident, walk in and take dinner at the Venus Restaurant, or loll on the benches in the Plaza, or rock in one of the great bent-wood chairs around the patio of the Don Carlos Club.

But, on the 27th of June, a long, yellow pit opened in the hill-side of San Juan, and in it we could see straw sombreros rising and bobbing up and down, and under the shade of the blockhouse, blue-coated Spaniards strolling leisurely about or riding forth on little white ponies to scamper over the hills. Officers of every regiment, attaches of foreign countries, correspondents, and staff officers daily reported the fact that the rifle-pits were growing in length and in number, and that in plain sight from the hill of El Poso the enemy was intrenching himself at San Juan, and at the little village of El Caney to the right, where he was marching through the streets. But no artillery was sent to El Poso hill to drop a shell among the busy men at work among the trenches, or to interrupt the street parades in El Caney. For four days before the American soldiers captured the same rifle-pits at El Caney and San Juan, with a loss of two thousand men, they watched these men diligently preparing for their coming, and wondered why there was no order to embarrass or to end these preparations.

On the afternoon of June 30, Captain Mills rode up to the tent of Colonel Wood, and told him that on account of illness, General Wheeler and General Young had relinquished their commands, and that General Sumner would take charge of the Cavalry Division; that he, Colonel Wood, would take command of General Young's brigade, and Colonel Carroll, of General

Sumner's brigade.

"You will break camp and move forward at four o'clock," he said. It was then three o'clock, and apparently the order to move forward at four had been given to each regiment at nearly the same time, for they all struck their tents and stepped down into the trail together. It was as though fifteen regiments were encamped along the sidewalks of Fifth Avenue and were all ordered at the same moment to move into it and march downtown. If Fifth Avenue were ten feet wide, one can imagine the confusion.

General Chaffee was at General Lawton's headquarters, and they stood apart whispering together about the march they were to take to El Caney. Just over their heads the balloon was ascending for the first time and its great glistening bulk hung just above the tree tops, and the men in different regiments, picking their way along the trail, gazed up at it open-mouthed. The head-quarters camp was crowded. After a week of inaction the army, at a moment's notice, was moving forward, and every one had ridden in haste to learn why.

There were attaches, in strange uniforms, self-important Cuban generals, officers from the flagship New York, and an army of photographers. At the side of the camp, double lines of soldiers passed slowly along the two paths of the muddy road, while, between them, aides dashed up and down, splashing them with dirty water, and shouting, "You will come up at once, sir." "You will not attempt to enter the trail yet, sir." "General Sumner's compliments, and why are you not in your place?"

Twelve thousand men, with their eyes fixed on a balloon, and treading on each other's heels in three inches of mud, move slowly, and after three hours, it seemed as though every man in the United States was under arms and stumbling and slipping down that trail. The lines passed until the moon rose. They seemed endless, interminable; there were cavalry mounted and dismounted, artillery with cracking whips and cursing drivers, Rough Riders in brown, and regulars, both black and white, in blue. Midnight came, and they were still stumbling and slipping forward.

General Sumner's head-quarters tent was pitched to the right of El Poso hill. Below us lay the basin a mile and a half in length, and a mile and a half wide, from which a white mist was rising. Near us, drowned under the mist, seven thousand men were sleeping, and, farther to the right, General Chaffee's five thousand were lying under the bushes along the trails to El Caney, waiting to march on it and eat it up before breakfast.

The place hardly needs a map to explain it. The trails were like a pitchfork, with its prongs touching the hills of San Juan. The long handle of the pitchfork was the trail over which we had just come, the joining of the handle and the prongs were El Poso. El Caney lay halfway along the right prong, the left one was the trail down which, in the morning, the troops were to be hurled upon San Juan. It was as yet an utterly undiscovered country. Three miles away, across the basin of mist, we could see the street lamps of Santiago shining over the San Juan hills. Above us, the tropical moon hung white and clear in the dark purple sky, pierced with millions of white stars. As we turned in, there was just a little something in the air which made saying "good-night" a gentle farce, for no one went to sleep immediately, but lay looking up at the stars, and after a long silence, and much restless turning on the blanket which we shared together, the second lieutenant said: "So, if anything happens to me, tomorrow, you'll see she gets them, won't you?" Before the moon rose again, every sixth man who had slept in the mist that night was either killed or wounded; but the second lieutenant was sitting on the edge of a Spanish rifle-pit, dirty, sweaty, and weak for food, but victorious, and the unknown she did not get them.

El Caney had not yet thrown off her blanket of mist before Capron's battery opened on it from a ridge two miles in the rear. The plan for the day was that El Caney should fall in an hour. The plan for the day is interesting chiefly because it is so different from what happened. According to the plan the army was to advance in two divisions along the two trails. Incidentally, General Lawton's division was to pick up El Caney, and when El Caney was eliminated, his division was to continue forward and join hands on the right with the divisions of General Sumner and General Kent. The army was then to rest for that night in the woods, half a mile from San Juan.

On the following morning it was to attack San Juan on the two flanks, under cover of artillery. The objection to this plan, which did not apparently suggest itself to General Shafter, was that an army of twelve thousand men, sleeping within five hundred yards of the enemy's rifle-pits, might not unreasonably be expected to pass a bad night. As we discovered the next day, not only the five hundred yards, but the whole basin was covered by the fire from the rifle-pits. Even by daylight, when it was possible to seek some slight shelter, the army could not remain in the woods, but according to the plan it was expected to bivouac for the night in those woods, and in the morning to manoeuvre and deploy and march through them to the two flanks of San Juan. How the enemy was to be hypnotized while this was going forward it is difficult to understand.

According to this programme, Capron's battery opened on El Caney and Grimes's battery opened on the pagoda-like block-house of San Juan. The range from El Poso was exactly 2,400 yards, and the firing, as was discovered later, was not very effective. The battery used black powder, and, as a result, after each explosion the curtain of smoke hung over the gun for fully a minute before the gunners could see the San Juan trenches, which was chiefly important because for a full minute it gave a mark to the enemy. The hill on which the battery stood was like a sugar-loaf. Behind it was the farm-house of El Poso, the only building in sight within a radius of a mile, and in it were Cuban soldiers and other non-combatants. The Rough Riders had been ordered to halt in the yard of the farm-house and the artillery horses were drawn up in it, under the lee of the hill. The First and Tenth dismounted Cavalry were encamped a hundred yards from the battery along the ridge. They might as sensibly have been ordered to paint the rings in a target while a company was firing at the bull's-eye. To our first twenty shots the enemy made no reply; when they did it was impossible, owing to their using smokeless powder, to locate their guns. Their third shell fell in among the Cubans in the block-house and among the Rough Riders and the men of the First and Tenth Cavalry, killing some and wounding many. These casualties were utterly unnecessary and were due to the stupidity of whoever placed the men within fifty yards of guns in action.

A quarter of an hour after the firing began from El Poso one of General Shafter's aides directed General Sumner to advance with his division down the Santiago trail, and to halt at the edge of the woods.

"What am I to do then?" asked General Sumner.

"You are to await further orders," the aide answered.

As a matter of fact and history this was probably the last order General Sumner received from General Shafter, until the troops of his division had taken the San Juan hills, as it became impossible to get word to General Shafter, the trail leading to his head-quarters tent, three miles in the rear, being blocked by the soldiers of the First and Tenth dismounted Cavalry, and later, by Lawton's division. General Sumner led the Sixth, Third, and Ninth Cavalry and the Rough Riders down the trail, with instructions for the First and Tenth to follow. The trail, virgin as yet from the foot of an American soldier, was as wide as its narrowest part, which was some ten feet across. At places it was as wide as Broadway, but only for such short distances that it was necessary for the men to advance in column, in double file. A maze of underbrush and trees on either side was all but impenetrable, and when the officers and men had once assembled into the basin, they could only guess as to what lay before them, or on either flank. At the end of a mile the country became more open, and General Sumner saw the Spaniards intrenched a half-mile away on the sloping hills. A stream, called the San Juan River, ran across the trail at this point, and another stream crossed it again two hundred yards farther on. The troops were halted at this first stream, some crossing it, and others deploying in single file to the right. Some were on the banks of the stream, others at the edge of the woods in the bushes. Others lay in the high grass which was so high that it stopped the wind, and so hot that it almost choked and suffocated those who lay in it.

The enemy saw the advance and began firing with pitiless accuracy into the jammed and crowded trail and along the whole border of the woods. There was not a single yard of ground for a mile to the rear which was not inside the zone of fire. Our men were ordered not to return the fire but to lie still and wait for further orders. Some of them could see the rifle-pits of the enemy quite clearly and the men in them, but many saw nothing but the bushes under which they lay, and the high grass which seemed to burn when they pressed against it. It was during this period of waiting that the greater number of our men were killed. For one hour they lay on their rifles staring at the waving green stuff around them, while the bullets drove past incessantly, with savage insistence, cutting the grass again and again in hundreds of fresh places. Men in line sprang from the ground and sank back again with a groan, or rolled to one side clinging silently to an arm or shoulder. Behind the lines hospital stewards passed continually, drawing the wounded back to the streams, where they laid them in long rows, their feet touching the water's edge and their bodies supported by the muddy bank. Up and down the lines, and through the fords of the streams, mounted aides drove their horses at a gallop, as conspicuous a target as the steeple on a church, and one after another paid the price of his position and fell from his horse wounded or dead. Captain Mills fell as he was giving an order, shot through the forehead behind both eyes; Captain O'Neill, of the Rough Riders, as he said, "There is no

Spanish bullet made that can kill me." Steel, Swift, Henry, each of them was shot out of his saddle.

Hidden in the trees above the streams, and above the trail, sharp-shooters and guerillas added a fresh terror to the wounded. There was no hiding from them. Their bullets came from every side. Their invisible smoke helped to keep their hiding-places secret, and in the incessant shriek of shrapnel and the spit of the Mausers, it was difficult to locate the reports of their rifles. They spared neither the wounded nor recognized the Red Cross; they killed the surgeons and the stewards carrying the litters, and killed the wounded men on the litters. A guerilla in a tree above us shot one of the Rough Riders in the breast while I was helping him carry Captain Morton Henry to the dressing-station, the ball passing down through him, and a second shot, from the same tree, barely missed Henry as he lay on the ground where we had dropped him. He was already twice wounded and so covered with blood that no one could have mistaken his condition. The surgeons at work along the stream dressed the wounds with one eye cast aloft at the trees. It was not the Mauser bullets they feared, though they passed continuously, but too high to do their patients further harm, but the bullets of the sharp-shooters which struck fairly in among them, splashing in the water and scattering the pebbles. The sounds of the two bullets were as different as is the sharp pop of a soda-water bottle from the buzzing of an angry wasp.

For a time it seemed as though every second man was either killed or wounded; one came upon them lying behind the bush, under which they had crawled with some strange idea that it would protect them, or crouched under the bank of the stream, or lying on their stomachs and lapping up the water with the eagerness of thirsty dogs. As to their suffering, the wounded were magnificently silent, they neither complained nor groaned nor cursed.

"I've got a punctured tire," was their grim answer to inquiries. White men and colored men, veterans and recruits and volunteers, each lay waiting for the battle to begin or to end so that he might be carried away to safety, for the wounded were in as great danger after they were hit as though they were in the firing line, but none questioned nor complained.

I came across Lieutenant Roberts, of the Tenth Cavalry, lying under the roots of a tree beside the stream with three of his colored troopers stretched around him. He was shot through the intestines, and each of the three men with him was shot in the arm or leg. They had been overlooked or forgotten, and we stumbled upon them only by the accident of losing our way. They had no knowledge as to how the battle was going or where their comrades were or where the enemy was. At any moment, for all they knew, the Spaniards might break through the bushes about them. It was a most lonely picture, the young lieutenant, half naked, and wet with his own blood, sitting upright beside the empty stream, and his three followers crouching at his feet like three faithful watch-dogs, each wearing his red badge of courage, with his black skin tanned to a haggard gray, and with his eyes fixed patiently on the white lips of his officer. When the white soldiers with me offered to carry him back to the dressing-station, the negroes resented it stiffly. "If the Lieutenant had been able to move, we would have carried him away long ago," said the sergeant, quite overlooking the fact that his arm was shattered.

"Oh, don't bother the surgeons about me," Roberts added, cheerfully. "They must be very busy. I can wait."

As yet, with all these killed and wounded, we had accomplished nothing - except to obey orders - which was to await further orders. The observation balloon hastened the end. It came blundering down the trail, and stopped the advance of the First and Tenth Cavalry, and was sent up directly over the heads of our men to observe what should have been observed a week before by scouts and reconnoitring parties. A balloon, two miles to the rear, and high enough in the air to be out of range of the enemy's fire may some day prove itself to be of use and value. But a balloon on the advance line, and only fifty feet above the tops of the trees, was merely an invitation to the enemy to kill everything beneath it. And the enemy responded to the invitation. A Spaniard might question if he could hit a man, or a number of men, hidden in the bushes, but had no doubt at all as to his ability to hit a mammoth glistening ball only six hundred yards distant, and so all the trenches fired at it at once, and the men of the First and Tenth, packed together directly behind it, received the full force of the bullets. The men lying directly below it received the shrapnel which was timed to hit it, and which at last, fortunately, did hit it. This was endured for an hour, an hour of such hell of fire and heat, that the heat in itself, had there been no bullets, would have been remembered for its cruelty. Men gasped on their backs, like fishes in the bottom of a boat, their heads burning inside and out, their limbs too heavy to move. They had been rushed here and rushed there wet with sweat and wet with fording the streams, under a sun that would have made moving a fan an effort, and they lay prostrate, gasping at the hot air, with faces aflame, and their tongues sticking out, and their eyes rolling. All through this the volleys from the rifle-pits sputtered and rattled, and the bullets sang continuously like the wind through the rigging in a gale, shrapnel whined and broke, and still no order came from General Shafter.

Captain Howse, of General Sumner's staff, rode down the trail to learn what had delayed the First and Tenth, and was hailed by Colonel Derby, who was just descending from the shattered balloon.

"I saw men up there on those hills," Colonel Derby shouted; "they are firing at our troops." That was part of the information contributed by the balloon. Captain Howse's reply is lost to history.

General Kent's division, which, according to the plan, was to have been held in reserve, had been rushed up in the rear of the First and Tenth, and the Tenth had deployed in skirmish order to the right. The trail was now completely blocked by Kent's division. Lawton's division, which was to have re-enforced on the right, had not appeared, but incessant firing from the direction of El Caney showed that he and Chaffee were fighting mightily. The situation was desperate. Our troops could not retreat, as the trail for two miles behind them was wedged with men. They could not remain where they were, for they were being shot to pieces. There was only one thing they could do - go forward and take the San Juan hills by assault. It was as desperate as the situation itself. To charge earthworks held by men with modern rifles, and using modern artillery, until after the earthworks have been shaken by artillery, and to attack them in advance and not in the flanks, are both impossible military propositions. But this campaign had not been conducted according to military rules, and a series of military blunders had brought seven thousand American soldiers into a chute of death from which there was no escape except by taking the enemy who held it by the throat and driving him out and beating him down. So the generals of divisions and brigades stepped back and relinquished their command to the regimental officers and the enlisted men.

"We can do nothing more," they virtually said. "There is the enemy."

Colonel Roosevelt, on horseback, broke from the woods behind the line of the Ninth, and finding its men lying in his way, shouted: "If you don't wish to go forward, let my men pass." The junior officers of the Ninth, with their negroes, instantly sprang into line with the Rough Riders, and charged at the blue block-house on the right.

I speak of Roosevelt first because, with General Hawkins, who led Kent's division, notably the Sixth and Sixteenth Regulars, he was, without doubt, the most conspicuous figure in the charge. General Hawkins, with hair as white as snow, and yet far in advance of men thirty years his junior, was so noble a sight that you felt inclined to pray for his safety; on the other hand, Roosevelt, mounted high on horseback, and charging the rifle-pits at a gallop and quite alone, made you feel that you would like to cheer. He wore on his sombrero a blue polka-dot handkerchief, a la Havelock, which, as he advanced, floated out straight behind his head, like a guidon. Afterward, the men of his regiment who followed this flag, adopted a polka-dot handkerchief as the badge of the Rough Riders.

These two officers were notably conspicuous in the charge, but no one can claim that any two men, or any one man, was more brave or more daring, or showed greater courage in that slow, stubborn advance, than did any of the others. Some one asked one of the officers if he had any difficulty in making his men follow him. "No," he answered, "I had some difficulty in keeping up with them." As one of the brigade generals said: "San Juan was won by the regimental officers and men. We had as little to do as the referee at a prize-fight who calls 'time.' We called 'time' and they did the fighting."

I have seen many illustrations and pictures of this charge on the San Juan hills, but none of them seem to show it just as I remember it. In the picture-papers the men are running uphill swiftly and gallantly, in regular formation, rank after rank, with flags flying, their eyes aflame, and their hair streaming, their bayonets fixed, in long, brilliant lines, an invincible, overpowering weight of numbers. Instead of which I think the thing which impressed one the most, when our men started from cover, was that they were so few. It seemed as if some one had made an awful and terrible mistake. One's instinct was to call to them to come back. You felt that some one had blundered and that these few men were blindly following out some madman's mad order. It was not heroic then, it seemed merely absurdly pathetic. The pity of it, the folly of such a sacrifice was what held you.

They had no glittering bayonets, they were not massed in regular array. There were a few men in advance, bunched together, and creeping up a steep, sunny hill, the tops of which roared and flashed with flame. The men held their guns pressed across their chests and stepped heavily as they climbed. Behind these first few, spreading out like a fan, were single lines of men, slipping and scrambling in the smooth grass, moving forward with difficulty, as though they were wading waist high through water, moving slowly, carefully, with strenuous effort. It was much more wonderful than any swinging charge could have been. They walked to greet death at every step, many of them, as they advanced, sinking suddenly or pitching forward and disappearing in the high grass, but the others waded on, stubbornly, forming a thin blue line that kept creeping higher and higher up the hill. It was as inevitable as the rising tide. It was a miracle of self-sacrifice, a triumph of bull-dog courage, which one watched breathless with wonder. The fire of the Spanish riflemen, who still stuck bravely to their posts, doubled and trebled in fierceness, the crests of the hills crackled and burst in amazed roars, and rippled with waves of tiny flame. But the blue line crept steadily up and on, and then, near the top, the broken fragments gathered together with a sudden burst of speed, the Spaniards appeared for a moment outlined against the sky and poised for instant flight, fired a last volley, and fled before the swift-moving wave that leaped and sprang after them.

The men of the Ninth and the Rough Riders rushed to the block-house together, the men of the Sixth, of the Third, of the Tenth Cavalry, of the Sixth and Sixteenth Infantry, fell on their faces along the crest of the hills beyond, and opened upon the vanishing enemy. They drove the yellow silk flags of the cavalry and the flag of their country into the soft earth of the trenches, and then sank down and looked back at the road they had climbed and swung their hats in the air. And from far overhead, from these few figures perched on the

Spanish rifle-pits, with their flags planted among the empty cartridges of the enemy, and overlooking the walls of Santiago, came, faintly, the sound of a tired, broken cheer.

III - THE TAKING OF COAMO

This is the inside story of the surrender, during the Spanish War, of the town of Coamo. It is written by the man to whom the town surrendered. Immediately after the surrender this same man became Military Governor of Coamo. He held office for fully twenty minutes.

Before beginning this story the reader must forget all he may happen to know of this particular triumph of the Porto Rican Expedition. He must forget that the taking of Coamo has always been credited to Major-General James H. Wilson, who on that occasion commanded Captain Anderson's Battery, the Sixteenth Pennsylvania, Troop C of Brooklyn, and under General Ernst, the Second and Third Wisconsin Volunteers. He must forget that in the records of the War Department all the praise, and it is of the highest, for this victory is bestowed upon General Wilson and his four thousand soldiers. Even the writer of this, when he cabled an account of the event to his paper, gave, with every one else, the entire credit to General Wilson. And ever since his conscience has upbraided him. His only claim for tolerance as a war correspondent has been that he always has stuck to the facts, and now he feels that in the sacred cause of history his friendship and admiration for General Wilson, that veteran of the Civil, Philippine, and Chinese Wars, must no longer stand in the way of his duty as an accurate reporter. He no longer can tell a lie. He must at last own up that he himself captured Coamo.

On the morning of the 9th of August, 1898, the Sixteenth Pennsylvania Volunteers arrived on the outskirts of that town. In order to get there they had spent the night in crawling over mountain trails and scrambling through streams and ravines. It was General Wilson's plan that by this flanking night march the Sixteenth Pennsylvania would reach the road leading from Coamo to San Juan in time to cut off the retreat of the Spanish garrison, when General Wilson, with the main body, attacked it from the opposite side.

At seven o'clock in the morning General Wilson began the frontal attack by turning loose the artillery on a block-house, which threatened his approach, and by advancing the Wisconsin Volunteers. The cavalry he sent to the right to capture Los Banos. At eight o'clock, from where the main body rested, two miles from Coamo, we could hear the Sixteenth Pennsylvania open its attack and instantly become hotly engaged. The enemy returned the fire fiercely, and the firing from both sides at once became so severe that it was evident the Pennsylvania Volunteers either would take the town without the main body, or that they would greatly need its assistance. The artillery was accordingly advanced one thousand yards and the infantry was hurried forward. The Second Wisconsin approached Coamo along the main road from Ponce, the Third Wisconsin through fields of grass to the right of the road, until the two regiments met at the ford by which the Banos road crosses the Coamo River. But before they met, from a position near the artillery, I had watched through my glasses the Second Wisconsin with General Ernst at its head advancing along the main road, and as, when I saw them, they were near the river, I guessed they would continue across the bridge and that they soon would be in the town.

As the firing from the Sixteenth still continued, it seemed obvious that General Ernst would be the first general officer to enter Coamo, and to receive its surrender. I had never seen five thousand people surrender to one man, and it seemed that, if I were to witness that ceremony, my best plan was to abandon the artillery and, as quickly as possible, pursue the Second Wisconsin. I did not want to share the spectacle of the surrender with my brother correspondents, so I tried to steal away from the three who were present. They were Thomas F. Millard, Walstein Root of the Sun, and Horace Thompson. By dodging through a coffee central I came out a half mile from them and in advance of the Third Wisconsin. There I encountered two "boy officers," Captain John C. Breckenridge and Lieutenant Fred. S. Titus, who had temporarily abandoned their thankless duties in the Commissariat Department in order to seek death or glory in the skirmish-line. They wanted to know where I was going, and when I explained, they declared that when Coamo surrendered they also were going to be among those present.

So we slipped away from the main body and rode off as an independent organization. But from the bald ridge, where the artillery was still hammering the town, the three correspondents and Captain Alfred Paget, Her Majesty's naval attache, observed our attempt to steal a march on General Wilson's forces, and pursued us and soon overtook us.

We now were seven, or to be exact, eight, for with Mr. Millard was "Jimmy," who in times of peace sells papers in Herald Square, and in times of war carries Mr. Millard's copy to the press post. We were much nearer the ford than the bridge, so we waded the "drift" and started on a gallop along the mile of military road that lay between us and Coamo. The firing from the Sixteenth Pennsylvania had slackened, but as we advanced it became sharper, more insistent, and seemed to urge us to greater speed. Across the road were dug rough rifle-pits which had the look of having been but that moment abandoned. What had been intended for the breakfast of the enemy was burning in pots over tiny fires, little heaps of cartridges lay in readiness upon the edges of each pit, and an arm-chair, in which a sentry had kept a comfortable lookout, lay sprawling in the middle of the road. The huts that faced it were empty. The only living things we saw were the chickens and pigs in the kitchen-gardens. On either hand was every evidence of hasty and panic-stricken flight. We rejoiced at these evidences of the fact that the Wisconsin Volunteers had swept all before them. Our rejoicings were not entirely unselfish. It was so quiet ahead that some one suggested the town had already surrendered. But that would have been too bitter a disappointment, and as the firing from the further side of Coamo still continued, we refused to believe it, and whipped the ponies into greater haste. We were now only a quarter of a mile distant from the built-up portion of Coamo, where the road turned sharply into the main street of the town.

Captain Paget, who in the absence of the British military attache on account of sickness, accompanied the army as a guest of General Wilson, gave way to thoughts of etiquette.

"Will General Wilson think I should have waited for him?" he shouted. The words were jolted out of him as he rose in the saddle. The noise of the ponies' hoofs made conversation difficult. I shouted back that the presence of General Ernst in the town made it quite proper for a foreign attache to enter it.

"It must have surrendered by now," I shouted. "It's been half an hour since Ernst crossed the bridge."

At these innocent words, all my companions tugged violently at their bridles and shouted "Whoa!"

"Crossed the bridge?" they yelled. "There is no bridge! The bridge is blown up! If he hasn't crossed by the ford, he isn't in the town!"

Then, in my turn, I shouted "Whoa!"

But by now the Porto Rican ponies had decided that this was the race of their lives, and each had made up his mind that, Mexican bit or no Mexican bit, until he had carried his rider first into the town of Coamo, he would not be halted. As I tugged helplessly at my Mexican bit, I saw how I had made my mistake. The volunteers, on finding the bridge destroyed, instead of marching upon Coamo had turned to the ford, the same ford which we had crossed half an hour before they reached it. They now were behind us. Instead of a town which had surrendered to a thousand American soldiers, we, seven unarmed men and Jimmy, were being swept into a hostile city as fast as the enemy's ponies could take us there.

Breckenridge and Titus hastily put the blame upon me.

"If we get into trouble with the General for this," they shouted, "it will be your fault. You told us Ernst was in the town with a thousand men."

I shouted back that no one regretted the fact that he was not more keenly than I did myself.

Titus and Breckenridge each glanced at a new, full-dress sword.

"We might as well go in," they shouted, "and take it anyway!" I decided that Titus and Breckenridge were wasted in the Commissariat Department.

The three correspondents looked more comfortable.

"If you officers go in," they cried, "the General can't blame us," and they dug their spurs into the ponies.

"Wait!" shouted Her Majesty's representative. "That's all very well for you chaps, but what protects me if the Admiralty finds out I have led a charge on a Spanish garrison?"

But Paget's pony refused to consider the feelings of the Lords of the Admiralty. As successfully Paget might have tried to pull back a row-boat from the edge of Niagara. And, moreover, Millard, in order that Jimmy might be the first to reach Ponce with despatches, had mounted him on the fastest pony in the bunch, and he already was far in the lead. His sporting instincts, nursed in the pool-rooms of the Tenderloin and at Guttenburg, had sent him three lengths to the good. It never would do to have a newsboy tell in New York that he had beaten the correspondents of the papers he sold in the streets; nor to permit commissioned officers to take the dust of one who never before had ridden on anything but a cable car. So we all raced forward and, bunched together, swept into the main street of Coamo. It was gratefully empty. There were no American soldiers, but, then, neither were there any Spanish soldiers. Across the street stretched more rifle-pits and barricades of iron pipes, but in sight there was neither friend nor foe. On the stones of the deserted street the galloping hoofs sounded like the advance of a whole regiment of cavalry. Their clatter gave us a most comfortable feeling. We almost could imagine the townspeople believing us to be the Rough Riders themselves and fleeing before us.

And then, the empty street seemed to threaten an ambush. We thought hastily of sunken mines, of soldiers crouching behind the barriers, behind the houses at the next corner, of Mausers covering us from the latticed balconies overhead. Until at last, when the silence had become alert and menacing, a lonely man dashed into the middle of the street, hurled a white flag in front of us, and then dived headlong under the porch of a house. The next instant, as though at a signal, a hundred citizens, each with a white flag in both hands, ran from cover, waving their banners, and gasping in weak and terror-shaken tones, "Vivan los Americanos."

We tried to pull up, but the ponies had not yet settled among themselves which of us had won, and carried us to the extreme edge of the town, where a precipice seemed to invite them to stop, and we fell off into the arms of the Porto Ricans. They brought us wine in tin cans, cigars, borne in the aprons and mantillas of their women-folk, and demijohns of native rum. They were abject, trembling, tearful. They made one instantly forget that the moment before he had been extremely frightened.

One of them spoke to me the few words of Spanish with which I had an acquaintance. He told me he was the Alcalde, and that he begged to surrender into my hands the town of Coamo. I led him instantly to one side. I was afraid that if I did not take him up he would surrender to Paget or to Jimmy. I bade him conduct me to his official residence. He did so, and gave me the key to the cartel, a staff of office of gold and ebony, and the flag of the town, which he had hidden behind his writing-desk. It was a fine Spanish flag with the coat of arms embroidered in gold. I decided that, with whatever else I might part, that flag would always be mine, that the chance of my again receiving the surrender of a town of five thousand people was slender, and that this token would be wrapped around me in my coffin. I accordingly hid it in my poncho and strapped it to my saddle. Then I appointed a hotel-keeper, who spoke a little English, as my official interpreter, and told the Alcalde that I was now Military Governor, Mayor, and Chief of Police, and that I wanted the seals of the town. He gave me a rubber stamp with a coat of arms cut in it, and I wrote myself three letters, which, to insure their safe arrival, I addressed to three different places, and stamped them with the rubber seals. In time all three reached me, and I now have them as documentary proof of the fact that for twenty minutes I was Military Governor and Mayor of Coamo.

During that brief administration I detailed Titus and Breckenridge to wigwag the Sixteenth Pennsylvania that we had taken the town, and that it was now safe for them to enter. In order to compromise Paget they used his red silk handkerchief. Root I detailed to conciliate the inhabitants by drinking with every one of them. He tells me he carried out my instructions to the letter. I also settled one assault and battery case, and put the chief offender under arrest. At least, I told the official interpreter to inform him that he was under arrest, but as I had no one to guard him he grew tired of being under arrest and went off to celebrate his emancipation from the rule of Spain.

My administration came to an end in twenty minutes, when General Wilson rode into Coamo at the head of his staff and three thousand men. He wore a white helmet, and he looked the part of the conquering hero so satisfactorily that I forgot I was Mayor and ran out into the street to snap a picture of him. He looked greatly surprised and asked me what I was doing in his town. The tone in which he spoke caused me to decide that, after all, I would not keep the flag of Coamo. I pulled it off my saddle and said: "General, it's too long a story to tell you now, but here is the flag of the town. It's the first Spanish flag" - and it was - "that has been captured in Porto Rico."

General Wilson smiled again and accepted the flag. He and about four thousand other soldiers think it belongs to them. But the truth will out. Some day the bestowal on the proper persons of a vote of thanks from Congress, a pension, or any other trifle, like prize-money, will show the American people to whom that flag really belongs.

I know that in time the glorious deed of the seven heroes of Coamo, or eight, if you include "Jimmy," will be told in song and story. Some one else will write the song. This is the story.

IV - THE PASSING OF SAN JUAN HILL

When I was a boy I thought battles were fought in waste places selected for the purpose. I argued from the fact that when our school nine wished to play ball it was forced into the suburbs to search for a vacant lot. I thought opposing armies also marched out of town until they reached some desolate spot where there were no window panes, and where their cannon-balls would hurt no one but themselves. Even later, when I saw battles fought among villages, artillery galloping through a cornfield, garden walls breached for rifle fire, and farm-houses in flames, it always seemed as though the generals had elected to fight in such surroundings through an inexcusable striving after theatrical effect - as though they wished to furnish the war correspondents with a chance for descriptive writing. With the horrors of war as horrible as they are without any aid from these contrasts, their presence always seemed not only sinful but bad art; as unnecessary as turning a red light on the dying gladiator.

There are so many places which are scenes set apart for battles - places that look as though Nature had condemned them for just such sacrifices. Colenso, with its bare kopjes and great stretch of veldt, is one of these, and so, also, is Spion Kop, and, in Manchuria, Nan Shan Hill. The photographs have made all of us familiar with the vast, desolate approaches to Port Arthur. These are among the waste places of the earth - barren, deserted, fit meeting grounds only for men whose object in life for the moment is to kill men. Were you shown over one of these places, and told, "A battle was fought here," you would answer, "Why, of course!"

But down in Cuba, outside of Santiago, where the United States army fought its solitary and modest battle with Spain, you might many times pass by San Juan Hill and think of it, if you thought of it at all, as only a pretty site for a bungalow, as a place obviously intended for orchards and gardens.

On July 1st, twelve years ago, when the American army came upon it out of the jungle the place wore a partial disguise. It still was an irregular ridge of smiling, sunny hills with fat, comfortable curves, and in some places a steep, straight front. But above the steepest, highest front frowned an aggressive block-house, and on all the slopes and along the sky-line were rows of yellow trenches, and at the base a cruel cat's cradle of barbed wire. It was like the face of a pretty woman behind the bars of a visor. I find that on the day of the fight twelve years ago I cabled my paper that San Juan Hill reminded the Americans of "a sunny orchard in New England." That was how it may have looked when the regulars were climbing up the steep front to capture the block-house, and when the cavalry and Rough Riders, having taken Kettle Hill, were running down its opposite slope, past the lake, to take that crest of San Juan Hill which lies to the right of the block-house. It may then have looked like a sunny New England orchard, but before night fell the intrenching tools had lent those sunny slopes "a fierce and terrible aspect." And after that, hour after hour, and day after day, we saw the hill eaten up by our trenches, hidden by a vast laundry of shelter tents, and torn apart by bomb-proofs, their jutting roofs of logs and broken branches weighed down by earth and stones and looking like the pit mouths to many mines. That probably is how most of the American army last saw San Juan Hill, and that probably is how it best remembers it - as a fortified camp. That was twelve years ago. When I revisited it, San Juan Hill was again a sunny, smiling farm land, the trenches planted with vegetables, the roofs of the bomb-proofs fallen in and buried beneath creeping vines, and the barbed-wire entanglements holding in check only the browsing cattle.

San Juan Hill is not a solitary hill, but the most prominent of a ridge of hills, with Kettle Hill a quarter of a mile away on the edge of the jungle and separated from the ridge by a tiny lake. In the local nomenclature Kettle Hill, which is the name given to it by the Rough Riders, has always been known as San Juan Hill, with an added name to distinguish it from the other San Juan Hill of greater renown.

The days we spent on those hills were so rich in incident and interest and were filled with moments of such excitement, of such pride in one's fellow-countrymen, of pity for the hurt and dying, of laughter and good-fellowship, that one supposed he might return after even twenty years and recognize every detail of the ground. But a shorter time has made startling and confusing changes. Now a visitor will find that not until after several different visits, and by walking and riding foot by foot over the hills, can he make them fall into line as he thinks he once knew them. Immediately around San Juan Hill itself there has been some attempt made to preserve the ground as a public park. A barbed-wire fence, with a gateway, encircles the block-house, which has been converted into a home for the caretaker of the park, and then, skirting the road to Santiago to include the tree under which the surrender was arranged, stretches to the left of the block-house to protect a monument. This monument was erected by Americans to commemorate the battle. It is now rapidly falling to pieces, but there still is enough of it intact to show the pencilled scribblings and autographs of tourists who did not take part in the battle, but who in this public manner show that they approve of its results. The public park is less than a quarter of a mile square. Except for it no other effort has been made either by Cubans or Americans to designate the lines that once encircled and menaced Santiago, and Nature, always at her best under a tropical sun, has done all in her power to disguise and forever obliterate the scene of the army's one battle. Those features which still remain unchanged are very few. The Treaty Tree, now surrounded by a tall fence, is one, the block-house is another. The little lake in which, even when the bullets were dropping, the men used to bathe and wash their clothes, the big iron sugar kettle that gave a new name to Kettle Hill, and here and there a trench hardly deeper than a ploughed furrow, and nearly hidden by growing plants, are the few landmarks that remain.

Of the camps of Generals Chaffee, Lawton, Bates, Sumner, and Wheeler, of Colonels Leonard Wood and Theodore Roosevelt, there are but the slightest traces. The Bloody Bend, as some call it, in the San Juan River, as some call that stream, seems to have entirely disappeared. At least, it certainly was not where it should have been, and the place the hotel guides point out to unsuspecting tourists bears not the slightest physical resemblance to that ford. In twelve years, during one of which there has been in Santiago the most severe rainfall in sixty years, the San Juan stream has carried away its banks and the trees that lined them, and the trails that should mark where the ford once crossed have so altered and so many new ones have been added, that the exact location of the once famous dressing station is now most difficult, if not impossible, to determine. To establish the sites of the old camping grounds is but little less difficult. The head-quarters of General Wheeler are easy to recognize, for the reason that the place selected was in a hollow, and the most unhealthy spot along the five miles of intrenchments. It is about thirty yards from where the road turns to rise over the ridge to Santiago, and all the water from the hill pours into it as into a rain barrel. It was here that Troop G, Third Cavalry, under Major Hardee, as it was Wheeler's escort, was forced to bivouac, and where one-third of its number came down with fever. The camp of General Sam Sumner was some sixty yards to the right of the head-quarters of General Wheeler, on the high shoulder of the hill just above the camp of the engineers, who were on the side of the road opposite. The camps of Generals Chaffee, Lawton, Hawkins, Ludlow, and the positions and trenches taken and held by the different regiments under them one can place only relatively. One reason for this is that before our army attacked the hills all the underbrush and small trees that might conceal the advance of our men had been cleared away by the Spaniards, leaving the hill, except for the high crest, comparatively bare. To-day the hills are thick with young trees and enormous bushes. The alteration in the landscape is as marked as is the difference between ground cleared for golf and the same spot planted with corn and fruit-trees.

Of all the camps, the one that to-day bears the strongest evidences of its occupation is that of the Rough Riders. A part of the camp of that regiment, which was situated on the ridge some hundred feet from the Santiago road, was pitched under a clump of shade trees, and to-day, even after seven years, the trunks of these trees bear the names and initials of the men who camped beneath them. {4} These men will remember that when they took this hill they found that the fortifications beneath the trees were partly made from the foundations of an adobe house. The red tiles from its roof still litter the ground. These tiles and the names cut in the bark of the trees determine absolutely the site of one-half of the camp, but the other half, where stood Tiffany's quick-firing gun and Parker's Gatling, has been almost obliterated. The tree under which Colonel pitched his tent I could not discover, and the trenches in which he used to sit with his officers and with the officers from the regiments of the regular army are now levelled to make a kitchen-garden. Sometimes the ex-President is said to have too generously given office and promotion to the friends he made in Cuba. These men he met in the trenches were then not necessarily his friends. To-day they are not necessarily his friends. They are the men the free life of the rifle-pits enabled him to know and to understand as the settled relations of home life and peace would never have permitted. At that time none of them guessed that the "amateur colonel," to whom they talked freely as to a comrade, would be their Commander-in-Chief. They did not suspect that he would become even the next Governor of New York, certainly not that in a few years he would be the

President of the United States. So they showed themselves to him frankly, unconsciously. They criticised, argued, disagreed, and he became familiar with the views, character, and worth of each, and remembered. The seeds planted in those half-obliterated trenches have borne greater results than ever will the kitchen-garden.

The kitchen-garden is immediately on the crest of the hill, and near it a Cuban farmer has built a shack of mud and twigs and cultivated several acres of land. On Kettle Hill there are three more such shacks, and over all the hills the new tenants have strung stout barbed-wire fences and made new trails and reared wooden gateways. It was curious to find how greatly these modern improvements confused one's recollection of the landscape, and it was interesting, also, to find how the presence on the hills of 12,000 men and the excitement of the time magnified distances and disarranged the landscape.

During the fight I walked along a portion of the Santiago road, and for many years I always have thought of that walk as extending over immense distances. It started from the top of San Juan Hill beside the block-house, where I had climbed to watch our artillery in action. By a mistake, the artillery had been sent there, and it remained exposed on the crest only about three minutes. During that brief moment the black powder it burned drew upon it the fire of every rifle in the Spanish line. To load his piece, each of our men was forced to crawl to it on his stomach, rise on one elbow in order to shove in the shell and lock the breech, and then, still flat on the ground, wriggle below the crest. In the three minutes three men were wounded and two killed; and the guns were withdrawn.

I also withdrew. I withdrew first. Indeed, all that happened after the first three seconds of those three minutes is hearsay, for I was in the Santiago road at the foot of the hill and retreating briskly. This road also was under a cross-fire, which made it stretch in either direction to an interminable distance. I remember a government teamster driving a Studebaker wagon filled with ammunition coming up at a gallop out of this interminable distance and seeking shelter against the base of the hill. Seated beside him was a small boy, freckled and sunburned, a stowaway from one of the transports. He was grandly happy and excited, and his only fear was that he was not "under fire." From our coign of safety, with our backs to the hill, the teamster and I assured him that, on that point, he need feel no morbid doubt. But until a bullet embedded itself in the blue board of the wagon he was not convinced. Then with his jack-knife he dug it out and shouted with pleasure. "I guess the folks will have to believe I was in a battle now," he said. That coign of safety ceasing to be a coign of safety caused us to move on in search of another, and I came upon Sergeant Borrowe blocking the road with his dynamite gun. He and his brother and three regulars were busily correcting a hitch in its mechanism. An officer carrying an order along the line halted his sweating horse and gazed at the strange gun with professional knowledge.

"That must be the dynamite gun I have heard so much about," he shouted. Borrowe saluted and shouted assent. The officer, greatly interested, forgot his errand.

"I'd like to see you fire it once," he said eagerly. Borrowe, delighted at the chance to exhibit his toy to a professional soldier, beamed with equal eagerness.

"In just a moment, sir," he said; "this shell seems to have jammed a bit." The officer, for the first time seeing the shell stuck in the breech, hurriedly gathered up his reins. He seemed to be losing interest. With elaborate carelessness I began to edge off down the road.

"Wait," Borrowe begged; "we'll have it out in a minute."

Suddenly I heard the officer's voice raised wildly.

"What - what," he gasped, "is that man doing with that axe?"

"He's helping me to get out this shell," said Borrowe.

"Good God!" said the officer. Then he remembered his errand.

Until last year, when I again met young Borrowe gayly disporting himself at a lawn-tennis tournament at Mattapoisett, I did not know whether his brother's method of removing dynamite with an axe had been entirely successful. He said it worked all right.

At the turn of the road I found Colonel Leonard Wood and a group of Rough Riders, who were busily intrenching. At the same moment Stephen Crane came up with "Jimmy" Hare, the man who has made the Russian-Japanese War famous. Crane walked to the crest and stood there as sharply outlined as a semaphore, observing the enemy's lines, and instantly bringing upon himself and us the fire of many Mausers. With every one else, Wood was crouched below the crest and shouted to Crane to lie down.

Crane, still standing, as though to get out of ear-shot, moved away, and Wood again ordered him to lie down.

"You're drawing the fire on these men," Wood commanded. Although the heat - it was the 1st of July in the tropics - was terrific, Crane wore a long India rubber rain-coat and was smoking a pipe. He appeared as cool as though he were looking down from a box at a theatre. I knew that to Crane, anything that savored of a pose was hateful, so, as I did not want to see him killed, I called, "You're not impressing any one by doing that, Crane." As I hoped he would, he instantly dropped to his knees. When he crawled over to where we lay, I explained, "I knew that would fetch you," and he grinned, and said, "Oh, was that it?"

A captain of the cavalry came up to Wood and asked permission to withdraw his troop from the top of the hill to a trench forty feet below the one they were in. "They can't possibly live where they are now," he explained, "and they're doing no good there, for they can't raise their heads to fire. In that lower trench they would be out of range themselves and would be able to fire back."

"Yes," said Wood, "but all the other men in the first trench would see them withdraw, and the moral effect would be bad. They needn't attempt to return the enemy's fire, but they must not retreat."

The officer looked as though he would like to argue. He was a West Point graduate and a full-fledged captain in the regular army. To him, Wood, in spite of his volunteer rank of colonel, which that day, owing to the illness of General Young, had placed him in command of a brigade, was still a doctor. But discipline was strong in him, and though he looked many things, he rose from his knees and grimly saluted. But at that moment, without waiting for the permission of any one, the men leaped out of the trench and ran. It looked as though they were going to run all the way to the sea, and the sight was sickening. But they had no intention of running to the sea. They ran only to the trench forty feet farther down and jumped into it, and instantly turning, began pumping lead at the enemy. Since five that morning Wood had been running about on his feet, his clothes stuck to him with sweat and the mud and water of forded streams, and as he rose he limped slightly. "My, but I'm tired!" he said, in a tone of the most acute surprise, and as though that fact was the only one that was weighing on his mind. He limped over to the trench in which the men were now busily firing off their rifles and waved a riding-crop he carried at the trench they had abandoned. He was standing as Crane had been standing, in silhouette against the sky-line. "Come back, boys," we heard him shouting. "The other men can't withdraw, and so you mustn't. It looks bad. Come on, get out of that!" What made it more amusing was that, although Wood had, like every one else, discarded his coat and wore a strange uniform of gray shirt, white riding-breeches, and a cowboy Stetson, with no insignia of rank, not even straps pinned to his shirt, still the men instantly accepted his authority. They looked at him on the crest of the hill, waving his stick persuasively at the grave-like trench at his feet, and then with a shout scampered back to it.

After that, as I had a bad attack of sciatica and no place to sleep and nothing to eat, I accepted Crane's offer of a blanket and coffee at his bivouac near El Poso. On account of the sciatica I was not able to walk fast, and, although for over a mile of the way the trail was under fire, Crane and Hare each insisted on giving me an arm, and kept step with my stumblings. Whenever I protested and refused their sacrifice and pointed out the risk they were taking they smiled as at the ravings of a naughty child, and when I lay down in the road and refused to budge unless they left me, Crane called the attention of Hare to the effect of the setting sun behind the palm-trees. To the reader all these little things that one remembers seem very little indeed, but they were vivid at the moment, and I have always thought of them as stretching over a long extent of time and territory. Before I revisited San Juan I would have said that the distance along the road from the point where I left the artillery to where I joined Wood was three-quarters of a mile. When I paced it later I found the distance was about seventy-five yards. I do not urge my stupidity or my extreme terror as a proof that others would be as greatly confused, but, if only for the sake of the stupid ones, it seems a pity that the landmarks of San Juan should not be rescued from the jungle, and a few sign-posts placed upon the hills. It is true that the great battles of the Civil War and those of the one in Manchuria, where the men killed and wounded in a day outnumber all those who fought on both sides at San Juan, make that battle read like a skirmish. But the Spanish War had its results. At least it made Cuba into a republic, and so enriched or burdened us with colonies that our republic changed into something like an empire. But I do not urge that. It will never be because San Juan changed our foreign policy that people will visit the spot, and will send from it picture postal cards. The human interest alone will keep San Juan alive. The men who fought there came from every State in our country and from every class of our social life. We sent there the best of our regular army, and with them, cowboys, clerks, bricklayers, foot-ball players, three future commanders of the greater army that followed that war, the future Governor of Cuba, future commanders of the Philippines, the commander of our forces in China, a future President of the United States. And, whether these men, when they returned to their homes again, became clerks and millionaires and dentists, or rose to be presidents and mounted policemen, they all remember very kindly the days they lay huddled together in the trenches on that hot and glaring sky-line. And there must be many more besides who hold the place in memory. There are few in the United States so poor in relatives and friends who did not in his or her heart send a substitute to Cuba. For these it seems as though San Juan might be better preserved, not as it is, for already its aspect is too far changed to wish for that, but as it was. The efforts already made to keep the place in memory and to honor the Americans who died there are the public park which I have mentioned, the monument on San Juan, and one other monument at Guasimas to the regulars and Rough Riders who were killed there. To these monuments the Society of Santiago will add four more, which will mark the landing place of the army at Daiquairi and the fights at Guasimas, El Caney, and San Juan Hill.

But I believe even more than this might be done to preserve to the place its proper values. These values are sentimental, historical, and possibly to the military student, educational. If to-day there were erected at Daiquairi, Siboney, Guasimas, El Poso, El Caney, and on and about San Juan a dozen iron or bronze tablets that would tell from where certain regiments advanced, what posts they held, how many or how few were the men who held those positions, how near they were to the trenches of the enemy, and by whom these men were commanded, I am sure the place would reconstruct itself and would breathe with interest, not only for the returning volunteer, but for any casual tourist. As it is, the history of the fight and the reputation of the men who fought is now at the mercy of the caretaker of the park and the Cuban "guides" from the hotel. The caretaker speaks only Spanish, and, considering the amount of misinformation the guides disseminate, it is a pity when they are talking to Americans, they are not forced to use the same language. When last I visited it, Carlos Portuondo was the official guardian of San Juan Hill. He is an aged Cuban, and he fought through the Ten Years' War, but during the last insurrection and the Spanish-American War he not only was not near San Juan, but was not even on the Island of Cuba. He is a charming old person, and so is his aged wife. Their chief concern in life, when I saw them, was to sell me a pair of breeches made of palm-fibre which Carlos had worn throughout the entire ten years of battle. The vicissitudes of those trousers he recited to me in great detail, and he very properly regarded them as of historic value. But of what happened at San Juan he knew nothing, and when I asked him why he held his present post and occupied the Block-House, he said, "To keep the cows out of the park." When I asked him where the Americans had camped, he pointed carefully from the back door of the Block-House to the foot of his kitchen-garden. I assured him that under no stress of terror could the entire American army have been driven into his back yard, and pointed out where it had stretched along the ridge of hills for five miles. He politely but unmistakably showed that he thought I was a liar. From the Venus Hotel there were two guides, old

Casanova and Jean Casanova, his languid and good-natured son, a youth of sixteen years. Old Casanova, like most Cubans, is not inclined to give much credit for what they did in Cuba to the Americans. After all, he says, they came only just as the Cubans themselves were about to conquer the Spaniards, and by a lucky chance received the surrender and then claimed all the credit. As other Cubans told me, "Had the Americans left us alone a few weeks longer, we would have ended the war." How they were to have taken Havana, and sunk Cervera's fleet, and why they were not among those present when our men charged San Juan, I did not inquire. Old Casanova, again like other Cubans, ranks the fighting qualities of the Spaniard much higher than those of the American. This is only human. It must be annoying to a Cuban to remember that after he had for three years fought the Spaniard, the Yankee in eight weeks received his surrender and began to ship him home. The way Casanova describes the fight at El Caney is as follows:

"The Americans thought they could capture El Caney in one day, but the brave General Toral fought so good that it was six days before the Americans could make the Spaniards surrender." The statement is correct except as regards the length of time during which the fight lasted. The Americans did make the mistake of thinking they could eat up El Caney in an hour and then march through it to San Juan. Owing to the splendid courage of Toral and his few troops our soldiers, under two of our best generals, were held in check from seven in the morning until two in the afternoon. But the difference between seven hours of one day and six days is considerable. Still, at present at San Juan that is the sort of information upon which the patriotic and puzzled American tourist is fed.

Young Casanova, the only other authority in Santiago, is not so sure of his facts as is his father, and is willing to learn. He went with me to hold my pony while I took the photographs that accompany this article, and I listened with great interest to his accounts of the battle. Finally he made a statement that was correct. "How did you happen to get that right?" I asked.

"Yesterday," he said, "I guided Colonel Hayes here, and while I guided him he explained it to me."

THE SOUTH AFRICAN WAR

I - WITH BULLER'S COLUMN

"Were you the station-master here before this?" I asked the man in the straw hat, at Colenso. "I mean before this war?"

"No fear!" snorted the station-master, scornfully. "Why, we didn't know Colenso was on the line until Buller fought a battle here. That's how it is with all these way-stations now. Everybody's talking about them. We never took no notice to them."

And yet the arriving stranger might have been forgiven his point of view and his start of surprise when he found Chieveley a place of only a half dozen corrugated zinc huts, and Colenso a scattered gathering of a dozen shattered houses of battered brick.

Chieveley seemed so insignificant in contrast with its fame to those who had followed the war on maps and in the newspapers, that one was not sure he was on the right road until he saw from the car-window the armored train still lying on the embankment, the graves beside it, and the donga into which Winston Churchill pulled and carried the wounded.

And as the train bumped and halted before the blue and

white enamel sign that marks Colenso station, the places which have made that spot familiar and momentous fell into line like the buoys which mark the entrance to a harbor.

We knew that the high bare ridge to the right must be Fort Wylie, that the plain on the left was where Colonel Long had lost his artillery, and three officers gained the Victoria Cross, and that the swift, muddy stream, in which the iron railroad bridge lay humped and sprawling, was the Tugela River.

Six hours before, at Frere Station, the station-master had awakened us to say that Ladysmith would be relieved at any moment. This had but just come over the wire. It was "official." Indeed, he added, with local pride, that the village band was still awake and in readiness to celebrate the imminent event. He found, I fear, an unsympathetic audience. The train was carrying philanthropic gentlemen in charge of stores of champagne and marmalade for the besieged city. They did not want it to be relieved until they were there to substitute pate de foie gras for horseflesh. And there were officers, too, who wanted a "look in," and who had been kept waiting at Cape Town for commissions, gladdening the guests of the Mount Nelson Hotel the while with their new khaki and gaiters, and there were Tommies who wanted "Relief of Ladysmith" on the claps of their medals, as they had seen "Relief of Lucknow" on the medals of the Chelsea pensioners. And there was a correspondent who had journeyed 15,000 miles to see Ladysmith relieved, and who was apparently going to miss that sight, after five weeks of travel, by a margin of five hours.

We all growled "That's good," as we had done for the

last two weeks every time we had heard it was relieved, but our tone was not enthusiastic. And when the captain of the Natal Carbineers said, "I am afraid the good news is too premature," we all said, hopefully, we were afraid it was.

We had seen nothing yet that was like real war. That night at Pietermaritzburg the officers at the hotel were in mess-jackets, the officers' wives in dinner-gowns. It was like Shepheard's Hotel, at the top of the season. But only six hours after that dinner, as we looked out of the car-windows, we saw galloping across the high grass, like men who had lost their way, and silhouetted black against the red sunrise, countless horsemen scouting ahead of our train, and guarding it against the fate of the armored one lying wrecked at Chieveley. The darkness was still heavy on the land and the only lights were the red eyes of the armored train creeping in advance of ours, and the red sun, which showed our silent escort appearing suddenly against the sky-line on a ridge, or galloping toward us through the dew to order us, with a wave of the hand, to greater speed. One hour after sunrise the train drew up at Colenso, and from only a mile away we heard the heavy thud of the naval guns, the hammering of the Boer "pom-poms," and the Maxims and Colt automatics spanking the air. We smiled at each other guiltily. We were on time. It was most evident that Ladysmith had not been relieved.

This was the twelfth day of a battle that Buller's column was waging against the Boers and their mountain ranges, or "disarranges," as some one described them, without having gained more than three miles of hostile territory. He had tried to force his way through them six times, and had been repulsed six times. And now he was to try it again.

No map, nor photograph, nor written description can give an idea of the country which lay between Buller and his goal. It was an eruption of high hills, linked together at every point without order or sequence. In most countries mountains and hills follow some natural law. The Cordilleras can be traced from the Amazon River to Guatemala City; they make the water-shed of two continents; the Great Divide forms the backbone of the States, but these Natal hills have no lineal descent. They are illegitimate children of no line, abandoned broadcast over the country, with no family likeness and no home. They stand alone, or shoulder to shoulder, or at right angles, or at a tangent, or join hands across a valley. They never appear the same; some run to a sharp point, some stretch out, forming a table-land, others are gigantic ant-hills, others perfect and accurately modelled ramparts. In a ride of half a mile, every hill completely loses its original aspect and character.

They hide each other, or disguise each other. Each can be enfiladed by the other, and not one gives up the secret of its strategic value until its crest has been carried by the bayonet. To add to this confusion, the river Tugela has selected the hills around Ladysmith as occupying the country through which it will endeavor to throw off its pursuers. It darts through them as though striving to escape, it doubles on its tracks, it sinks out of sight between them, and in the open plain rises to the dignity of water-falls. It runs uphill, and remains motionless on an incline, and on the level ground twists and turns so frequently that when one says he has crossed the Tugela, he means he has crossed it once at a drift, once at the wrecked railroad bridge, and once over a pontoon. And then he is not sure that he is not still on the same side from which he started.

Some of these hills are green, but the greater part are a yellow or dark red, against which at two hundred yards a man in khaki is indistinguishable from the rocks around him. Indeed, the khaki is the English soldier's sole protection. It saves him in spite of himself, for he apparently cannot learn to advance under cover, and a sky-line is the one place where he selects to stand erect and stretch his weary limbs. I have come to within a hundred yards of a hill before I saw that scattered among its red and yellow bowlders was the better part of a regiment as closely packed together as the crowd on the bleaching boards at a base-ball match.

Into this maze and confusion of nature's fortifications Buller's column has been twisting and turning, marching and countermarching, capturing one position after another, to find it was enfiladed from many hills, and abandoning it, only to retake it a week later. The greater part of the column has abandoned its tents and is bivouacking in the open. It is a wonderful and impressive sight. At the first view, an army in being, when it is spread out as it is in the Tugela basin back of the hills, seems a hopelessly and irrevocably entangled mob.

An army in the field is not regiments of armed men, marching with a gun on shoulder, or crouching behind trenches. That is the least, even if it seems the most, important part of it. Before one reaches the firing-line he must pass villages of men, camps of men, bivouacs of men, who are feeding, mending, repairing, and burying the men at the "front." It is these latter that make the mob of gypsies, which is apparently without head or order or organization. They stretched across the great basin of the Tugela, like the children of Israel, their camp-fires rising to the sky at night like the reflection of great search-lights; by day they swarmed across the plain, like hundreds of moving circus-vans in every direction, with as little obvious intention as herds of buffalo. But each had his appointed work, and each was utterly indifferent to the battle going forward a mile away. Hundreds of teams, of sixteen oxen each, crawled like great black water-snakes across the drifts, the Kaffir drivers, naked and black, lashing them with whips as long as lariats, shrieking, beseeching, and howling, and falling upon the oxen's horns to drag them into place.

Mules from Spain and Texas, loaded with ammunition, kicked and plunged, more oxen drew more soberly the great naval guns, which lurched as though in a heavy sea, throwing the blue-jackets who hung upon the drag-ropes from one high side of the trail to the other. Across the plain, and making toward the trail, wagons loaded with fodder, with rations, with camp equipment, with tents and cooking-stoves, crowded each other as closely as cable-cars on Broadway. Scattered among them were fixed lines of tethered horses, rows of dog-tents, camps of Kaffirs, hospital stations with the Red Cross waving from the nearest and highest tree. Dripping water-carts with as many spigots as the regiment had companies, howitzer guns guided by as many ropes as a May-pole, crowded past these to the trail, or gave way to the ambulances filled with men half dressed and bound in the zinc-blue bandages that made the color detestable forever after. Troops of the irregular horse gallop through this multitude, with a jangling of spurs and sling-belts; and

Tommies, in close order, fight their way among the oxen, or help pull them to one side as the stretchers pass, each with its burden, each with its blue bandage stained a dark brownish crimson. It is only when the figure on the stretcher lies under a blanket that the tumult and push and sweltering mass comes to a quick pause, while the dead man's comrade stands at attention, and the officer raises his fingers to his helmet. Then the mass surges on again, with cracking of whips and shouts and imprecations, while the yellow dust rises in thick clouds and buries the picture in a glaring fog. This moving, struggling mass, that fights for the right of way along the road, is within easy distance of the shells. Those from their own guns pass over them with a shrill crescendo, those from the enemy burst among them at rare intervals, or sink impotently in the soft soil. And a dozen Tommies rush to dig them out as keepsakes. Up at the front, brown and yellow regiments are lying crouched behind brown and yellow rocks and stones. As far as you can see, the hills are sown with them. With a glass you distinguish them against the sky-line of every hill, for over three miles away. Sometimes the men rise and fire, and there is a feverish flutter of musketry; sometimes they lie motionless for hours while the guns make the ways straight.

Any one who has seen Epsom Downs on a Derby day, with its thousands of vans and tents and lines of horses and moving mobs, can form some idea of what it is like. But while at the Derby all is interest and excitement, and every one is pushing and struggling, and the air palpitates with the intoxication of a great event, the winning of a horse-race - here, where men are killed every hour and no one of them knows when his turn may come, the fact that most impresses you is their indifference to it all. What strikes you most is the bored air of the Tommies, the undivided interest of the engineers in the construction of a pontoon bridge, the solicitude of the medical staff over the long lines of wounded, the rage of the naked Kaffirs at their lumbering steers; the fact that every one is intent on something - anything - but the battle.

They are wearied with battles. The Tommies stretch themselves in the sun to dry the wet khaki in which they have lain out in the cold night for weeks, and yawn at battles. Or, if you climb to the hill where the officers are seated, you will find men steeped even deeper in boredom. They are burned a dark red; their brown mustaches look white by contrast, theirs are the same faces you have met with in Piccadilly, which you see across the tables of the Savoy restaurant, which gaze depressedly from the windows of White's and the Bachelors' Club. If they were bored then, they are unbearably bored now. Below them the men of their regiment lie crouched amid the bowlders, hardly distinguishable from the brown and yellow rock. They are sleeping, or dozing, or yawning. A shell passes over them like the shaking of many telegraph wires, and neither officer nor Tommy raises his head to watch it strike. They are tired in body and in mind, with cramped limbs and aching eyes. They have had twelve nights and twelve days of battle, and it has lost its power to amuse.

When the sergeants call the companies together, they are eager enough. Anything is better than lying still looking up at the sunny, inscrutable hills, or down into the plain crawling with black oxen.

Among the group of staff officers some one has lost a

cigar-holder. It has slipped from between his fingers, and, with the vindictiveness of inanimate things, has slid and jumped under a pile of rocks. The interest of all around is instantly centred on the lost cigar-holder. The Tommies begin to roll the rocks away, endangering the limbs of the men below them, and half the kopje is obliterated. They are as keen as terriers after a rat. The officers sit above and give advice and disagree as to where that cigar-holder hid itself. Over their heads, not twenty feet above, the shells chase each other fiercely. But the officers have become accustomed to shells; a search for a lost cigar-holder, which is going on under their very eyes, is of greater interest. And when at last a Tommy pounces upon it with a laugh of triumph, the officers look their disappointment, and, with a sigh of resignation, pick up their field-glasses.

It is all a question of familiarity. On Broadway, if a building is going up where there is a chance of a loose brick falling on some one's head, the contractor puts up red signs marked "Danger!" and you dodge over to the other side. But if you had been in battle for twelve days, as have the soldiers of Buller's column, passing shells would interest you no more than do passing cable-cars. After twelve days you would forget that shells are dangerous even as you forget when crossing Broadway that cable-cars can kill and mangle.

Up on the highest hill, seated among the highest rocks, are General Buller and his staff. The hill is all of rocks, sharp, brown rocks, as clearly cut as foundation-stones. They are thrown about at irregular angles, and are shaded only by stiff bayonet-like cacti. Above is a blue glaring sky, into which the top of the kopje seems to reach, and to draw and concentrate upon itself all of the sun's heat. This little jagged point of blistering rocks holds the forces that press the button which sets the struggling mass below, and the thousands of men upon the surrounding hills, in motion. It is the conning tower of the relief column, only, unlike a conning tower, it offers no protection, no seclusion, no peace. To-day, commanding generals, under the new conditions which this war has developed, do not charge up hills waving flashing swords. They sit on rocks, and wink out their orders by a flashing hand-mirror. The swords have been left at the base, or coated deep with mud, so that they shall not flash, and with this column every one, under the rank of general, carries a rifle on purpose to disguise the fact that he is entitled to carry a sword. The kopje is the central station of the system. From its uncomfortable eminence the commanding general watches the developments of his attack, and directs it by heliograph and ragged bits of bunting. A sweating, dirty Tommy turns his back on a hill a mile away and slaps the air with his signal flag; another Tommy, with the front visor of his helmet cocked over the back of his neck, watches an answering bit of bunting through a glass. The bit of bunting, a mile away, flashes impatiently, once to the right and once to the left, and the Tommy with the glass says, "They understand, sir," and the other Tommy, who has not as yet cast even an interested glance at the regiment he has ordered into action, folds his flag and curls up against a hot rock and instantly sleeps.

Stuck on the crest, twenty feet from where General Buller is seated, are two iron rods, like those in the putting-green of a golf course. They mark the line of direction which a shell must take, in order to seek out the enemy. Back of the kopje, where they cannot see the enemy, where they cannot even see the hill upon which he is intrenched, are the howitzers. Their duty is to aim at the iron rods, and vary their aim to either side of them as they are directed to do by an officer on the crest. Their shells pass a few yards over the heads of the staff, but the staff has confidence. Those three yards are as safe a margin as a hundred. Their confidence is that of the lady in spangles at a music-hall, who permits her husband in buckskin to shoot apples from the top of her head. From the other direction come the shells of the Boers, seeking out the hidden howitzers. They pass somewhat higher, crashing into the base of the kopje, sometimes killing, sometimes digging their own ignominious graves. The staff regard them with the same indifference. One of them tears the overcoat upon which Colonel Stuart-Wortley is seated, another destroys his diary. His men, lying at his feet among the red rocks, observe this with wide eyes. But he does not shift his position. His answer is, that his men cannot shift theirs.

On Friday, February 23d, the Inniskillings, Dublins, and Connaughts were sent out to take a trench, half-way up Railway Hill. The attack was one of those frontal attacks, which in this war, against the new weapons, have added so much to the lists of killed and wounded and to the prestige of the men, while it has, in an inverse ratio, hurt the prestige of the men by whom the attack was ordered. The result of this attack was peculiarly disastrous. It was made at night, and as soon as it developed, the Boers retreated to the trenches on the crest of the hill, and threw men around the sides to bring a cross-fire to bear on the Englishmen. In the morning the Inniskillings found they had lost four hundred men, and ten out of their fifteen officers. The other regiments lost as heavily. The following Tuesday, which was the anniversary of Majuba Hill, three brigades, instead of a regiment, were told off to take this same Railway Hill, or Pieter's, as it was later called, on the flank, and with it to capture two others. On the same day, nineteen years before, the English had lost Majuba Hill, and their hope was to take these three from the Boers for the one they had lost, and open the way to Bulwana Mountain, which was the last bar that held them back from Ladysmith.

The first two of the three hills they wanted were shoulder to shoulder, the third was separated from them by a deep ravine. This last was the highest, and in order that the attack should be successful, it was necessary to seize it first. The hills stretched for three miles; they were about one thousand two hundred yards high.

For three hours a single line of men slipped and stumbled forward along the muddy bank of the river, and for three hours the artillery crashed, spluttered, and stabbed at the three hills above them, scattering the rocks and bursting over and behind the Boer trenches on the crest.

As is their custom, the Boers remained invisible and made no reply. And though we knew they were there, it seemed inconceivable that anything human could live under such a bombardment of shot, bullets, and shrapnel. A hundred yards distant, on our right, the navy guns were firing lyddite that burst with a thick yellow smoke; on the other side Colt automatics were put-put-put-ing a stream of bullets; the field-guns and the howitzers were playing from a hill half a mile behind us, and scattered among the rocks about us, and for two miles on either hand, the infantry in reserve were firing off ammunition at any part of the three hills they happened to dislike!

The roar of the navy's Four-Point-Sevens, their crash, their rush as they passed, the shrill whine of the shrapnel, the barking of the howitzers, and the mechanical, regular rattle of the quick-firing Maxims, which sounded like the clicking of many mowing-machines on a hot summer's day, tore the air with such hideous noises that one's skull ached from the concussion, and one could only be heard by shouting. But more impressive by far than this hot chorus of mighty thunder and petty hammering, was the roar of the wind which was driven down into the valley beneath, and which swept up again in enormous waves of sound. It roared like a wild hurricane at sea. The illusion was so complete, that you expected, by looking down, to see the Tugela lashing at her banks, tossing the spray hundreds of feet in air, and battling with her sides of rock. It was like the roar of Niagara in a gale, and yet when you did look below, not a leaf was stirring, and the Tugela was slipping forward, flat and sluggish, and in peace.

The long procession of yellow figures was still advancing along the bottom of the valley, toward the right, when on the crest of the farthermost hill fourteen of them appeared suddenly, and ran forward and sprang into the trenches.

Perched against the blue sky on the highest and most distant of the three hills, they looked terribly lonely and insufficient, and they ran about, this way and that, as though they were very much surprised to find themselves where they were. Then they settled down into the Boer trench, from our side of it, and began firing, their officer, as his habit is, standing up behind them. The hill they had taken had evidently been abandoned to them by the enemy, and the fourteen men in khaki had taken it by "default." But they disappeared so suddenly into the trench, that we knew they were not enjoying their new position in peace, and every one looked below them, to see the arriving reinforcements. They came at last, to the number of ten, and scampered about just as the others had done, looking for cover. It seemed as if we could almost hear the singing of the bullet when one of them dodged, and it was with a distinct sense of relief, and of freedom from further responsibility, that we saw the ten disappear also, and become part of the yellow stones about them. Then a very wonderful movement began to agitate the men upon the two remaining hills. They began to creep up them as you have seen seaweed rise with the tide and envelop a rock. They moved in regiments, but each man was as distinct as is a letter of the alphabet in each word on this page, black with letters. We began to follow the fortunes of individual letters. It was a most selfish and cowardly occupation, for you knew you were in no greater danger than you would be in looking through the glasses of a mutoscope. The battle unrolled before you like a panorama. The guns on our side of the valley had ceased, the hurricane in the depths below had instantly spent itself, and the birds and insects had again begun to fill our hill with drowsy twitter and song. But on the other, half the men were wrapping the base of the hill in khaki, which rose higher and higher, growing looser and less tightly wrapt as it spun upward. Halfway to the crest there was a broad open space of green grass, and above that a yellow bank of earth, which supported the track of the railroad. This green space spurted with tiny geysers of yellow dust. Where the bullets came from or who sent them we could not see. But the loose ends of the bandage of khaki were stretching across this green space and the yellow spurts of dust rose all around them. The men crossed this fire zone warily, looking to one side or the other, as the bullets struck the earth heavily, like drops of rain before a shower.

The men had their heads and shoulders bent as though they thought a roof was about to fall on them; some ran from rock to rock, seeking cover properly; others scampered toward the safe vantage-ground behind the railroad embankment; others advanced leisurely, like men playing golf. The silence, after the hurricane of sounds, was painful; we could not hear even the Boer rifles. The men moved like figures in a dream, without firing a shot. They seemed each to be acting on his own account, without unison or organization. As I have said, you ceased considering the scattered whole, and became intent on the adventures of individuals. These fell so suddenly, that you waited with great anxiety to learn whether they had dropped to dodge a bullet or whether one had found them. The men came at last from every side, and from out of every ridge and dried-up waterway. Open spaces which had been green a moment before were suddenly dyed yellow with them. Where a company had been clinging to the railroad embankment, there stood one regiment holding it, and another sweeping over it. Heights that had seemed the goal, became the resting-place of the stretcher-bearers, until at last no part of the hill remained unpopulated, save a high bulging rampart of unprotected and open ground. And then, suddenly, coming from the earth itself, apparently, one man ran across this open space and leaped on top of the trench which crowned the hill. He was fully fifteen yards in advance of all the rest, entirely unsupported, and alone. And he had evidently planned it so, for he took off his helmet and waved it, and stuck it on his rifle and waved it again, and then suddenly clapped it on his head and threw his gun to his shoulder. He stood so, pointing down into the trench, and it seemed as though we could hear him calling upon the Boers behind it to surrender.

A few minutes later the last of the three hills was mounted by the West Yorks, who were mistaken by their own artillery for Boers, and fired upon both by the Boers and by their own shrapnel and lyddite. Four men were wounded, and, to save themselves, a line of them stood up at full length on the trench and cheered and waved at the artillery until it had ceased to play upon them. The Boers continued to fire upon them with rifles for over two hours. But it was only a demonstration to cover the retreat of the greater number, and at daybreak the hills were in complete and peaceful possession of the English.

These hills were a part of the same Railway Hill which four nights before the Inniskillings and a composite regiment had attempted to take by a frontal attack with the loss of six hundred men, among whom were three colonels. By this flank attack, and by using nine regiments instead of one, the same hills and two others were taken with two hundred casualties. The fact that this battle, which was called the Battle of Pieter's Hill, and the surrender of General Cronje and his forces to Lord Roberts, both took place on the anniversary of the battle of Majuba Hill, made the whole of Buller's column feel that the ill memory of that disaster had been effaced.

II - THE RELIEF OF LADYSMITH

After the defeat of the Boers at the battle of Pieter's Hill there were two things left for them to do. They could fall back across a great plain which stretched from Pieter's Hill to Bulwana Mountain, and there make their last stand against Buller and the Ladysmith relief column, or they could abandon the siege of Ladysmith and slip away after having held Buller at bay for three months.

Bulwana Mountain is shaped like a brick and blocks the valley in which Ladysmith lies. The railroad track slips around one end of the brick, and the Dundee trail around the other. It was on this mountain that the Boers had placed their famous gun, Long Tom, with which they began the bombardment of Ladysmith, and with which up to the day before Ladysmith was relieved they had thrown three thousand shells into that miserable town.

If the Boers on retreating from Pieter's Hill had fortified this mountain with the purpose of holding off Buller for a still longer time, they would have been under a fire from General White's artillery in the town behind them and from Buller's naval guns in front. Their position would not have been unlike that of Humpty Dumpty on the wall, so they wisely adopted the only alternative and slipped away. This was on

Tuesday night, while the British were hurrying up artillery to hold the hills they had taken that afternoon.

By ten o'clock the following morning from the top of Pieter's Hill you could still see the Boers moving off along the Dundee road. It was an easy matter to follow them, for the dust hung above the trail in a yellow cloud, like mist over a swamp. There were two opinions as to whether they were halting at Bulwana or passing it, on their way to Laing's Neck. If they were going only to Bulwana there was the probability of two weeks' more fighting before they could be dislodged. If they had avoided Bulwana, the way to Ladysmith was open.

Lord Dundonald, who is in command of a brigade of irregular cavalry, was scouting to the left of Bulwana, far in advance of our forces. At sunset he arrived, without having encountered the Boers, at the base of Bulwana. He could either return and report the disappearance of the enemy or he could make a dash for it and enter Ladysmith. His orders were "to go, look, see," and avoid an action, and the fact that none of his brigade was in the triumphant procession which took place three days later has led many to think that in entering the besieged town without orders he offended the commanding general. In any event, it is a family row and of no interest to the outsider. The main fact is that he did make a dash for it, and just at sunset found himself with two hundred men only a mile from the "Doomed City." His force was composed of Natal Carbiniers and Imperial Light Horse. He halted them, and in order that honors might be even, formed them in sections with the half sections made up from each of the two organizations. All the officers were placed in front, and with a cheer they started to race across the plain.

The wig-waggers on Convent Hill had already seen them, and the townspeople and the garrison were rushing through the streets to meet them, cheering and shouting, and some of them weeping. Others, so officers tell me, who were in the different camps, looked down upon the figures galloping across the plain in the twilight, and continued making tea.

Just as they had reached the centre of the town, General Sir George White and his staff rode down from head-quarters and met the men whose coming meant for him life and peace and success. They were advancing at a walk, with the cheering people hanging to their stirrups, clutching at their hands and hanging to the bridles of their horses.

General White's first greeting was characteristically unselfish and loyal, and typical of the British officer. He gave no sign of his own in calculable relief, nor did he give to Caesar the things which were Caesar's. He did not cheer Dundonald, nor Buller, nor the column which had rescued him and his garrison from present starvation and probable imprisonment at Pretoria. He raised his helmet and cried, "We will give three cheers for the Queen!" And then the general and the healthy, ragged, and sunburned troopers from the outside world, the starved, fever-ridden garrison, and the starved, fever-ridden civilians stood with hats off and sang their national anthem.

The column outside had been fighting steadily for six weeks to get Dundonald or any one of its force into Ladysmith; for fourteen days it had been living in the open, fighting by night as well as by day, without halt or respite; the garrison inside had been for four months holding the enemy at bay with the point of the bayonet; it was famished for food, it was rotten with fever, and yet when the relief came and all turned out well, the first thought of every one was for the Queen!

It may be credulous in them or old-fashioned; but it is certainly very unselfish, and when you take their point of view it is certainly very fine.

After the Queen every one else had his share of the cheering, and General White could not complain of the heartiness with which they greeted him, he tried to make a speech in reply, but it was a brief one. He spoke of how much they owed to General Buller and his column, and he congratulated his own soldiers on the defence they had made.

"I am very sorry, men," he said, "that I had to cut down your rations. I - I promise you I won't do it again."

Then he stopped very suddenly and whirled his horse's head around and rode away. Judging from the number of times they told me of this, the fact that they had all but seen an English general give way to his feelings seemed to have impressed the civilian mind of Ladysmith more than the entrance of the relief force. The men having come in and demonstrated that the way was open, rode forth again, and the relief of Ladysmith had taken place. But it is not the people cheering in the dark streets, nor General White breaking down in his speech of welcome, which gives the note to the way the men of Ladysmith received their freedom. It is rather the fact that as the two hundred battle-stained and earth-stained troopers galloped forward, racing to be the first, and rising in their stirrups to cheer, the men in the hospital camps said, "Well, they're come at last, have they?" and continued fussing over their fourth of a ration of tea. That gives the real picture of how Ladysmith came into her inheritance, and of how she received her rescuers.

On the morning after Dundonald had ridden in and out of Ladysmith, two other correspondents and myself started to relieve it on our own account. We did not know the way to Ladysmith, and we did not then know whether or not the Boers still occupied Bulwana Mountain. But we argued that the chances of the Boers having raised the siege were so good that it was worth risking their not having done so, and being taken prisoner.

We carried all the tobacco we could pack in our saddle-bags, and enough food for one day. My chief regret was that my government, with true republican simplicity, had given me a passport, type-written on a modest sheet of notepaper and wofully lacking in impressive seals and coats of arms. I fancied it would look to Boer eyes like one I might have forged for myself in the writing-room of the hotel at Cape Town.

We had ridden up Pieter's Hill and scrambled down on its other side before we learned that the night before Dundonald had raised the siege. We learned this from long trains of artillery and regiments of infantry which already were moving forward over the great plain which lies between Pieter's and Bulwana. We learned it also from the silence of conscientious, dutiful correspondents, who came galloping back as we galloped forward, and who made wide detours at sight of us, or who, when we hailed them, lashed their ponies over the red rocks and pretended not to hear, each unselfishly turning his back on Ladysmith in the hope that he might be the first to send word that the "Doomed City" was relieved. This would enable one paper to say that it had the news "on the street" five minutes earlier than its hated rivals. We found that the rivalry of our respective papers bored us. We condemned it as being childish and weak. London, New York, Chicago were names, they were spots thousands of leagues away: Ladysmith was just across that mountain. If our horses held out at the pace, we would be - after Dundonald - the first men in. We imagined that we would see hysterical women and starving men. They would wring our hands, and say, "God bless you," and we would halt our steaming horses in the market-place, and distribute the news of the outside world, and tobacco. There would be shattered houses, roofless homes, deep pits in the roadways where the shells had burst and buried themselves. We would see the entombed miner at the moment of his deliverance, we would be among the first from the outer world to break the spell of his silence; the first to receive the brunt of the imprisoned people's gratitude and rejoicings.

Indeed, it was clearly our duty to the papers that employed us that we should not send them news, but that we should be the first to enter Ladysmith. We were surely the best judges of what was best to do. How like them to try to dictate to us from London and New York, when we were on the spot! It was absurd. We shouted this to each other as we raced in and out of the long confused column, lashing viciously with our whips. We stumbled around pieces of artillery, slid in between dripping water-carts, dodged the horns of weary oxen, scattered companies of straggling Tommies, and ducked under protruding tent-poles on the baggage-wagons, and at last came out together again in advance of the dusty column.

"Besides, we don't know where the press-censor is, do we?" No, of course we had no idea where the press-censor was, and unless he said that Ladysmith was relieved, the fact that twenty-five thousand other soldiers said so counted for idle gossip. Our papers could not expect us to go riding over mountains the day Ladysmith was relieved, hunting for a press-censor. "That press-censor," gasped Hartland, "never - is - where he - ought to be." The words were bumped out of him as he was shot up and down in the saddle. That was it. It was the press-censor's fault. Our consciences were clear now. If our papers worried themselves or us because they did not receive the great news until every one else knew of it, it was all because of that press-censor. We smiled again and spurred the horses forward. We abused the press-censor roundly - we were extremely indignant with him. It was so like him to lose himself the day Ladysmith was relieved. "Confound him," we muttered, and grinned guiltily. We felt as we used to feel when we were playing truant from school.

We were nearing Pieter's Station now, and were half-way to Ladysmith. But the van of the army was still about us. Was it possible that it stretched already into the beleaguered city? Were we, after all, to be cheated of the first and freshest impressions? The tall lancers turned at the sound of the horses' hoofs and stared, infantry officers on foot smiled up at us sadly, they were dirty and dusty and sweating, they carried rifles and cross belts like the Tommies; and they knew that we outsiders who were not under orders would see the chosen city before them. Some of them shouted to us, but we only nodded and galloped on. We wanted to get rid of them all, but they were interminable. When we thought we had shaken them off, and that we were at last in advance, we would come upon a group of them resting on the same ground their shells had torn up during the battle the day before.

We passed Boer laagers marked by empty cans and broken saddles and black, cold campfires. At Pieter's Station the blood was still fresh on the grass where two hours before some of the South African Light Horse had been wounded.

The Boers were still on Bulwana then? Perhaps, after all, we had better turn back and try to find that press-censor. But we rode on and saw Pieter's Station, as we passed it, as an absurd relic of by-gone days when bridges were intact and trains ran on schedule time. One door seen over the shoulder as we galloped past read, "Station Master's Office - Private," and in contempt of that stern injunction, which would make even the first-class passenger hesitate, one of our shells had knocked away the half of the door and made its privacy a mockery. We had only to follow the track now and we would arrive in time - unless the Boers were still on Bulwana. We had shaken off the army, and we were two miles in front of it, when six men came galloping toward us in an unfamiliar uniform. They passed us far to the right, regardless of the trail, and galloping through the high grass. We pulled up when we saw them, for they had green facings to their gray uniforms, and no one with Buller's column wore green facings.

We gave a yell in chorus. "Are you from Ladysmith?" we shouted. The men, before they answered, wheeled and cheered, and came toward us laughing jubilant. "We're the first men out," cried the officer and we rode in among them, shaking hands and offering our good wishes. "We're glad to see you," we said. "We're glad to see YOU," they said. It was not an original greeting, but it seemed sufficient to all of us. "Are the Boers on Bulwana?" we asked. "No, they've trekked up Dundee way. You can go right in."

We parted at the word and started to go right in. We found the culverts along the railroad cut away and the bridges down, and that galloping ponies over the roadbed of a railroad is a difficult feat at the best, even when the road is in working order.

Some men, cleanly dressed and rather pale-looking, met us and said: "Good-morning." "Are you from Ladysmith?" we called. "No, we're from the neutral camp," they answered. We were the first men from outside they had seen in four months, and that was the extent of their interest or information. They had put on their best clothes, and were walking along the track to Colenso to catch a train south to Durban or to Maritzburg, to any place out of the neutral camp. They might have been somnambulists for all they saw of us, or of the Boer trenches and the battle-field before them. But we found them of greatest interest, especially their clean clothes. Our column had not seen clean linen in six weeks, and the sight of these civilians in white duck and straw hats, and carrying walking-sticks, coming toward us over the railroad ties, made one think it was Sunday at home and these were excursionists to the suburbs.

We had been riding through a roofless tunnel, with the mountain and the great dam on one side, and the high wall of the railway cutting on the other, but now just ahead of us lay the open country, and the exit of the tunnel barricaded by twisted rails and heaped-up ties and bags of earth. Bulwana was behind us. For eight miles it had shut out the sight of our goal, but now, directly in front of us, was spread a great city of dirty tents and grass huts and Red Cross flags - the neutral camp - and beyond that, four miles away, shimmering and twinkling sleepily in the sun, the white walls and zinc roofs of Ladysmith.

We gave a gasp of recognition and galloped into and through the neutral camp. Natives of India in great turbans, Indian women in gay shawls and nose-rings, and black Kaffirs in discarded khaki looked up at us dully from the earth floors of their huts, and when we shouted "Which way?" and "Where is the bridge?" only stared, or pointed vaguely, still staring.

After all, we thought, they are poor creatures, incapable of emotion. Perhaps they do not know how glad we are that they have been rescued. They do not understand that we want to shake hands with everybody and offer our congratulations. Wait until we meet our own people, we said, they will understand! It was such a pleasant prospect that we whipped the unhappy ponies into greater bursts of speed, not because they needed it, but because we were too excited and impatient to sit motionless.

In our haste we lost our way among innumerable little trees; we disagreed as to which one of the many cross-trails led home to the bridge. We slipped out of our stirrups to drag the ponies over one steep place, and to haul them up another, and at last the right road lay before us, and a hundred yards ahead a short iron bridge and a Gordon Highlander waited to welcome us, to receive our first greetings and an assorted collection of cigarettes. Hartland was riding a thoroughbred polo pony and passed the gallant defender of Ladysmith without a kind look or word, but Blackwood and I galloped up more decorously, smiling at him with good-will. The soldier, who had not seen a friend from the outside world in four months, leaped in front of us and presented a heavy gun and a burnished bayonet.

"Halt, there," he cried. "Where's your pass?" Of course it showed excellent discipline - we admired it immensely. We even overlooked the fact that he should think Boer spies would enter the town by way of the main bridge and at a gallop. We liked his vigilance, we admired his discipline, but in spite of that his reception chilled us. We had brought several things with us that we thought they might possibly want in Ladysmith, but we had entirely forgotten to bring a pass. Indeed I do not believe one of the twenty-five thousand men who had been fighting for six weeks to relieve Ladysmith had supplied himself with one. The night before, when the Ladysmith sentries had tried to halt Dundonald's troopers in the same way, and demanded a pass from them, there was not one in the squadron.

We crossed the bridge soberly and entered Ladysmith at a walk. Even the ponies looked disconcerted and crestfallen. After the high grass and the mountains of red rock, where there was not even a tent to remind one of a roof-tree, the stone cottages and shop-windows and chapels and well-ordered hedges of the main street of Ladysmith made it seem a wealthy and attractive suburb. When we entered, a Sabbath-like calm hung upon the town; officers in the smartest khaki and glistening Stowassers observed us askance, little girls in white pinafores passed us with eyes cast down, a man on a bicycle looked up, and then, in terror lest we might speak to him, glued his eyes to the wheel and "scorched" rapidly. We trotted forward and halted at each street crossing, looking to the right and left in the hope that some one might nod to us. From the opposite end of the town General Buller and his staff came toward us slowly - the house-tops did not seem to sway - it was not "roses, roses all the way." The German army marching into Paris received as hearty a welcome. "Why didn't you people cheer General Buller when he came in?" we asked later. "Oh, was that General Buller?" they inquired. "We didn't recognize him." "But you knew he was a general officer, you knew he was the first of the relieving column?" "Ye-es, but we didn't know who he was."

I decided that the bare fact of the relief of Ladysmith was all I would be able to wire to my neglected paper, and with remorses started to find the Ladysmith censor. Two officers, with whom I ventured to break the hush that hung upon the town by asking my way, said they were going in the direction of the censor. We rode for some distance in guarded silence. Finally, one of them, with an inward struggle, brought himself to ask, "Are you from the outside?"

I was forced to admit that I was. I felt that I had taken an unwarrantable liberty in intruding on a besieged garrison. I wanted to say that I had lost my way and had ridden into the town by mistake, and that I begged to be allowed to withdraw with apologies. The other officer woke up suddenly and handed me a printed list of the prices which had been paid during the siege for food and tobacco. He seemed to offer it as being in some way an official apology for his starved appearance. The price of cigars struck me as especially pathetic, and I commented on it. The first officer gazed mournfully at the blazing sunshine before him. "I have not smoked a cigar in two months," he said. My surging sympathy, and my terror at again offending the haughty garrison, combated so fiercely that it was only with a great effort that I produced a handful. "Will you have these?" The other officer started in his saddle so violently that I thought his horse had stumbled, but he also kept his eyes straight in front. "Thank you, I will take one if I may - just one," said the first officer. "Are you sure I am not robbing you?" They each took one, but they refused to put the rest of the cigars in their pockets. As the printed list stated that a dozen matches sold for $1.75, I handed them a box of matches. Then a beautiful thing happened. They lit the cigars and at the first taste of the smoke - and they were not good cigars - an almost human expression of peace and good-will and utter abandonment to joy spread over their yellow skins and cracked lips and fever-lit eyes. The first man dropped his reins and put his hands on his hips and threw back his head and shoulders and closed his eyelids. I felt that I had intruded at a moment which should have been left sacred. {5}

Another boy officer in stainless khaki and beautifully turned out, polished and burnished and varnished, but with the same yellow skin and sharpened cheek-bones and protruding teeth, a skeleton on horse-back, rode slowly toward us down the hill. As he reached us he glanced up and then swayed in his saddle, gazing at my companions fearfully. "Good God," he cried. His brother officers seemed to understand, but made no answer, except to jerk their heads toward me. They were too occupied to speak. I handed the skeleton a cigar, and he took it in great embarrassment, laughing and stammering and blushing. Then I began to understand; I began to appreciate the heroic self-sacrifice of the first two, who, when they had been given the chance, had refused to fill their pockets. I knew then that it was an effort worthy of the V. C.

The censor was at his post, and a few minutes later a signal officer on Convent Hill heliographed my cable to Bulwana, where, six hours after the Boers had abandoned it, Buller's own helios had begun to dance, and they speeded the cable on its long journey to the newspaper office on the Thames Embankment.

When one descended to the streets again - there are only two streets which run the full length of the town - and looked for signs of the siege, one found them not in the shattered houses, of which there seemed surprisingly few, but in the starved and fever-shaken look of the people.

The cloak of indifference which every Englishman wears, and his instinctive dislike to make much of his feelings, and, in this case, his pluck, at first concealed from us how terribly those who had been inside of Ladysmith had suffered, and how near to the breaking point they were. Their faces were the real index to what they had passed through.

Any one who had seen our men at Montauk Point or in the fever camp at Siboney needed no hospital list to tell him of the pitiful condition of the garrison. The skin on their faces was yellow, and drawn sharply over the brow and cheekbones; their teeth protruded, and they shambled along like old men, their voices ranging from a feeble pipe to a deep whisper. In this pitiable condition they had been forced to keep night-watch on the hill-crests, in the rain, to lie in the trenches, and to work on fortifications and bomb-proofs. And they were expected to do all of these things on what strength they could get from horse-meat, biscuits of the toughness and composition of those that are fed to dogs, and on "mealies," which is what we call corn.

That first day in Ladysmith gave us a faint experience as to what the siege meant. The correspondents had disposed of all their tobacco, and within an hour saw starvation staring them in the face, and raced through the town to rob fellow-correspondents who had just arrived. The new-comers in their turn had soon distributed all they owned, and came tearing back to beg one of their own cigarettes. We tried to buy grass for our ponies, and were met with pitying contempt; we tried to buy food for ourselves, and were met with open scorn. I went to the only hotel which was open in the place, and offered large sums for a cup of tea.

"Put up your money," said the Scotchman in charge, sharply. "What's the good of your money? Can your horse eat money? Can you eat money? Very well, then, put it away."

The great dramatic moment after the raising of the siege was the entrance into Ladysmith of the relieving column. It was a magnificent, manly, and moving spectacle. You must imagine the dry, burning heat, the fine, yellow dust, the white glare of the sunshine, and in the heat and glare and dust the great interminable column of men in ragged khaki crowding down the main street, twenty-two thousand strong, cheering and shouting, with the sweat running off their red faces and cutting little rivulets in the dust that caked their cheeks.

Some of them were so glad that, though in the heaviest marching order, they leaped up and down and stepped out of line to dance to the music of the bagpipes. For hours they crowded past, laughing, joking, and cheering, or staring ahead of them, with lips wide apart, panting in the heat and choking with the dust, but always ready to turn again and wave their helmets at Sir George White.

It was a pitiful contrast which the two forces presented. The men of the garrison were in clean khaki, pipe-clayed and brushed and polished, but their tunics hung on them as loosely as the flag around its pole, the skin on their cheek-bones was as tight and as yellow as the belly of a drum, their teeth protruded through parched, cracked lips, and hunger, fever, and suffering stared from out their eyes. They were so ill and so feeble that the mere exercise of standing was too severe for their endurance, and many of them collapsed, falling back to the sidewalk, rising to salute only the first troop of each succeeding regiment. This done, they would again sink back and each would sit leaning his head against his musket, or with his forehead resting heavily on his folded arms. In comparison the relieving column looked like giants as they came in with a swinging swagger, their uniforms blackened with mud and sweat and bloodstains, their faces brilliantly crimsoned and blistered and tanned by the dust and sun. They made a picture of strength and health and aggressiveness. Perhaps the contrast was strongest when the battalion of the Devons that had been on foreign service passed the "reserve" battalion which had come from England. The men of the two battalions had parted five years before in India, and they met again in Ladysmith, with the men of one battalion lining the streets, sick, hungry, and yellow, and the others, who had been fighting six weeks to reach it, marching toward them, robust, red-faced, and cheering mightily. As they met they gave a shout of recognition, and the men broke ranks and ran forward, calling each other by name, embracing, shaking hands, and punching each other in the back and shoulders. It was a sight that very few men watched unmoved. Indeed, the whole three hours was one of the most brutal assaults upon the feelings that it has been my lot to endure. One felt he had been entirely lifted out of the politics of the war, and the question of the wrongs of the Boers disappeared before a simple propostiton of brave men saluting brave men.

Early in the campaign, when his officers had blundered, General White had dared to write: "I alone am to blame." But in this triumphal procession twenty-two thousand gentlemen in khaki wiped that line off the slate, and wrote, "Well done, sir," in its place, as they passed before him through the town he had defended and saved.

III - THE NIGHT BEFORE THE BATTLE

The Boer "front" was at Brandfort, and, as Lord Roberts was advancing upon that place, one already saw in the head-lines, "The Battle of Brandfort." But before our train drew out of Pretoria Station we learned that the English had just occupied Brandfort, and that the Boer front had been pushed back to Winburg.

We decided that Brandfort was an impossible position to hold anyway, and that we had better leave the train at Winburg. We found some selfish consolation for the Boer repulse, in the fact that it shortened our railroad journey by one day. The next morning when we awoke at the Vaal River Station the train despatcher informed us that during the night the "Rooineks" had taken Winburg, and that the burghers were gathered at Smaaldel.

We agreed not to go to Winburg, but to stop off at Smaaldel. We also agreed that Winburg was an impossible position to hold. When at eleven o'clock the train reached Kroonstad, we learned than Lord Roberts was in Smaaldel. It was then evident that if our train kept on and the British army kept on there would be a collision. So we stopped at Kroonstad. In talking it over we decided that, owing to its situation, Smaaldel was an impossible position to hold.

The Sand River, which runs about forty miles south of Kroonstad, was the last place in the Free State at which the burghers could hope to make a stand, and at the bridge where the railroad spans the river, and at a drift ten miles lower down, the Boers and Free Staters had collected to the number of four thousand. Lord Roberts and his advancing column, which was known to contain thirty-five thousand men, were a few miles distant from the opposite bank of the Sand River. There was an equal chance that the English would attempt to cross at the drift or at the bridge. We thought they would cross at the drift, and stopped for the night at Ventersburg, a town ten miles from the river.

Ventersburg, in comparison with Kroonstad, where we had left them rounding up stray burghers and hurrying them to the firing-line, and burning official documents in the streets, was calm.

Ventersburg was not destroying incriminating documents nor driving weary burghers from its solitary street. It was making them welcome at Jones's Hotel. The sun had sunk an angry crimson, the sure sign of a bloody battle on the morrow, and a full moon had turned the dusty street and the veldt into which it disappeared into a field of snow.

The American scouts had halted at Jones's Hotel, and the American proprietor was giving them drinks free. Their cowboy spurs jingled on the floor of the bar-room, on the boards of the verandas, on the stone floor of the kitchen, and in the billiard-room, where they were playing pool as joyously as though the English were not ten miles away. Grave, awkward burghers rode up, each in a cloud of dust, and leaving his pony to wander in the street and his rifle in a corner, shook hands with every one solemnly, and asked for coffee. Italians of Garibaldi's red-shirted army, Swedes and Danes in semi-uniform, Frenchman in high boots and great sombreros, Germans with the sabre cuts on their cheeks that had been given them at the university, and Russian officers smoking tiny cigarettes crowded the little dining-room, and by the light of a smoky lamp talked in many tongues of Spion Kop, Sannahspost, Fourteen Streams, and the battle on the morrow.

They were sun-tanned, dusty, stained, and many of them with wounds in bandages. They came from every capital of Europe, and as each took his turn around the crowded table, they drank to the health of every nation, save one. When they had eaten they picked up the pony's bridle from the dust and melted into the moonlight with a wave of the hand and a "good luck to you." There were no bugles to sound "boots and saddles" for them, no sergeants to keep them in hand, no officers to pay for their rations and issue orders.

Each was his own officer, his conscience was his bugle-call, he gave himself orders. They were all equal, all friends; the cowboy and the Russian Prince, the French socialist from La Villette or Montmartre, with a red sash around his velveteen breeches, and the little French nobleman from the Cercle Royal who had never before felt the sun, except when he had played lawn tennis on the Isle de Puteaux. Each had his bandolier and rifle; each was minding his own business, which was the business of all - to try and save the independence of a free people.

The presence of these foreigners, with rifle in hand, showed the sentiment and sympathies of the countries from which they came. These men were Europe's real ambassadors to the Republic of the Transvaal. The hundreds of thousands of their countrymen who had remained at home held toward the Boer the same feelings, but they were not so strongly moved; not so strongly as to feel that they must go abroad to fight.

These foreigners were not the exception in opinion, they were only exceptionally adventurous, exceptionally liberty-loving. They were not soldiers of fortune, for the soldier of fortune fights for gain. These men receive no pay, no emolument, no reward. They were the few who dared do what the majority of their countrymen in Europe thought.

At Jones's Hotel that night, at Ventersburg, it was as though a jury composed of men from all of Europe and the United States had gathered in judgment on the British nation.

Outside in the moonlight in the dusty road two bearded burghers had halted me to ask the way to the house of the commandant. Between them on a Boer pony sat a man, erect, slim-waisted, with well-set shoulders and chin in air, one hand holding the reins high, the other with knuckles down resting on his hip. The Boer pony he rode, nor the moonlight, nor the veldt behind him, could disguise his seat and pose. It was as though I had been suddenly thrown back into London and was passing the cuirassed, gauntleted guardsman, motionless on his black charger in the sentry gate in Whitehall. Only now, instead of a steel breastplate, he shivered through his thin khaki, and instead of the high boots, his legs were wrapped in twisted putties.

"When did they take you?" I asked.

"Early this morning. I was out scouting," he said. He spoke in a voice so well trained and modulated that I tried to see his shoulder-straps.

"Oh, you are an officer?" I said.

"No, sir, a trooper. First Life Guards."

But in the moonlight I could see him smile, whether at my mistake or because it was not a mistake I could not guess. There are many gentlemen rankers in this war.

He made a lonely figure in the night, his helmet marking him as conspicuously as a man wearing a high hat in a church. From the billiard-room, where the American scouts were playing pool, came the click of the ivory and loud, light-hearted laughter; from the veranda the sputtering of many strange tongues and the deep, lazy voices of the Boers. There were Boers to the left of him, Boers to the right of him, pulling at their long, drooping pipes and sending up big rings of white smoke in the white moonlight.

He dismounted, and stood watching the crowd about him under half-lowered eyelids, but as unmoved as though he saw no one. He threw his arm over the pony's neck and pulled its head down against his chest and began talking to it.

It was as though he wished to emphasize his loneliness.

"You are not tired, are you? No, you're not," he said. His voice was as kindly as though he were speaking to a child.

"Oh, but you can't be tired. What?" he whispered. "A little hungry, perhaps. Yes?" He seemed to draw much comfort from his friend the pony, and the pony rubbed his head against the Englishman's shoulder.

"The commandant says he will question you in the morning. You will come with us to the jail now," his captor directed. "You will find three of your people there to talk to. I will go bring a blanket for you, it is getting cold." And they rode off together into the night.

Two days later he would have heard through the windows of Jones's Hotel the billiard balls still clicking joyously, but the men who held the cues then would have worn helmets like his own.

The original Jones, the proprietor of Jones's Hotel, had fled. The man who succeeded him was also a refugee, and the present manager was an American from Cincinnati. He had never before kept a hotel, but he confided to me that it was not a bad business, as he found that on each drink sold he made a profit of a hundred per cent. The proprietress was a lady from Brooklyn, her husband, another American, was a prisoner with Cronje at St. Helena. She was in considerable doubt as to whether she ought to run before the British arrived, or wait and chance being made a prisoner. She said she would prefer to escape, but what with standing on her feet all day in the kitchen preparing meals for hungry burghers and foreign volunteers, she was too tired to get away.

War close at hand consists so largely of commonplaces and trivial details that I hope I may be pardoned for recording the anxieties and cares of this lady from Brooklyn. Her point of view so admirably illustrates one side of war. It is only when you are ten years away from it, or ten thousand miles away from it, that you forget the dull places, and only the moments loom up which are terrible, picturesque, and momentous. We have read, in "Vanity Fair," of the terror and the mad haste to escape of the people of Brussels on the eve of Waterloo. That is the obvious and dramatic side.

That is the picture of war you remember and which appeals. As a rule, people like to read of the rumble of cannon through the streets of Ventersburg, the silent, dusty columns of the re-enforcements passing in the moonlight, the galloping hoofs of the aides suddenly beating upon the night air and growing fainter and dying away, the bugle-calls from the camps along the river, the stamp of spurred boots as the general himself enters the hotel and spreads the blue-print maps upon the table, the clanking sabres of his staff, standing behind him in the candle-light, whispering and tugging at their gauntlets while the great man plans his attack. You must stop with the British army if you want bugle-calls and clanking sabres and gauntlets. They are a part of the panoply of war and of warriors. But we saw no warriors at Ventersburg that night, only a few cattle-breeders and farmers who were fighting for the land they had won from the lion and the bushman, and with them a mixed company of gentleman adventurers - gathered around a table discussing other days in other lands. The picture of war which is most familiar is the one of the people of Brussels fleeing from the city with the French guns booming in the distance, or as one sees it in "Shenandoah," where aides gallop on and off the stage and the night signals flash from both sides of the valley. That is the obvious and dramatic side; the other side of war is the night before the battle, at Jones's Hotel; the landlady in the dining-room with her elbows on the table, fretfully deciding that after a day in front of the cooking-stove she is too tired to escape an invading army, declaring that the one place at which she would rather be at that moment was Green's restaurant in Philadelphia, the heated argument that immediately follows between the foreign legion and the Americans as to whether Rector's is not better than the Cafe de Paris, and the general agreement that Ritz cannot hope to run two hotels in London without being robbed. That is how the men talked and acted on the eve of a battle. We heard no galloping aides, no clanking spurs, only the click of the clipped billiard balls as the American scouts (who were killed thirty-six hours later) knocked them about the torn billiard-cloth, the drip, drip of the kerosene from a blazing, sweating lamp, which struck the dirty table-cloth, with the regular ticking of a hall clock, and the complaint of the piano from the hotel parlor, where the correspondent of a Boston paper was picking out "Hello, My Baby," laboriously with one finger. War is not so terribly dramatic or exciting - at the time; and the real trials of war - at the time, and not as one later remembers them - consist largely in looting fodder for your ponies and in bribing the station-master to put on an open truck in which to carry them.

We were wakened about two o'clock in the morning by a loud knocking on a door and the distracted voice of the local justice of the peace calling upon the landlord to rouse himself and fly. The English, so the voice informed the various guests, as door after door was thrown open upon the court-yard, were at Ventersburg Station, only two hours away. The justice of the peace wanted to buy or to borrow a horse, and wanted it very badly, but a sleepy-eyed and sceptical audience told him unfeelingly that he was either drunk or dreaming, and only the landlady, now apparently refreshed after her labors, was keenly, even hysterically, intent on instant flight. She sat up in her bed with her hair in curl papers and a revolver beside her, and through her open door shouted advice to her lodgers. But they were unsympathetic, and reassured her only by banging their doors and retiring with profane grumbling, and in a few moments the silence was broken only by the voice of the justice as he fled down the main street of Ventersburg offering his kingdom for a horse.

The next morning we rode out to the Sand River to see the Boer positions near the drift, and met President Steyn in his Cape cart coming from them on his way to the bridge. Ever since the occupation of Bloemfontein, the London papers had been speaking of him as "the Late President," as though he were dead. He impressed me, on the contrary, as being very much alive and very much the President, although his executive chamber was the dancing-hall of a hotel and his roof-tree the hood of a Cape cart. He stood in the middle of the road, and talked hopefully of the morrow. He had been waiting, he said, to see the development of the enemy's attack, but the British had not appeared, and, as he believed they would not advance that day, he was going on to the bridge to talk to his burghers and to consult with General Botha. He was much more a man of the world and more the professional politician than President Kruger. I use the words "professional politician" in no unpleasant sense, but meaning rather that he was ready, tactful, and diplomatic. For instance, he gave to whatever he said the air of a confidence reserved especially for the ear of the person to whom he spoke. He showed none of the bitterness which President Kruger exhibits toward the British, but took the tone toward the English Government of the most critical and mused tolerance. Had he heard it, it would have been intensely annoying to any Englishman.

"I see that the London Chronicle," he said, "asks if, since I have become a rebel, I do not lose my rights as a Barrister of the Temple? Of course, we are no more rebels than the Spaniards were rebels against the United States. By a great stretch of the truth, under the suzerainty clause, the burghers of the Transvaal might be called rebels, but a Free Stater - never! It is not the animosity of the English which I mind," he added, thoughtfully, "but their depressing ignorance of their own history."

His cheerfulness and hopefulness, even though one guessed they were assumed, commanded one's admiration. He was being hunted out of one village after another, the miles of territory still free to him were hourly shrinking - in a few days he would be a refugee in the Transvaal; but he stood in the open veldt with all his possessions in the cart behind him, a president without a republic, a man without a home, but still full of pluck, cheerful and unbeaten.

The farm-house of General Andrew Cronje stood just above the drift and was the only conspicuous mark for the English guns on our side of the river, so in order to protect it the general had turned it over to the ambulance corps to be used as a hospital. They had lashed a great Red Cross flag to the chimney and filled the clean shelves of the generously built kitchen with bottles of antiseptics and bitter-smelling drugs and surgeons' cutlery. President Steyn gave me a letter to Dr. Rodgers Reid, who was in charge, and he offered us our choice of the deserted bedrooms. It was a most welcome shelter, and in comparison to the cold veldt the hospital was a haven of comfort. Hundreds of cooing doves, stumbling over the roof of the barn, helped to fill the air with their peaceful murmur. It was a strange overture to a battle, but in time I learned to not listen for any more martial prelude. The Boer does not make a business of war, and when he is not actually fighting he pretends that he is camping out for pleasure. In his laager there are no warlike sounds, no sentries challenge, no bugles call. He has no duties to perform, for his Kaffir boys care for his pony, gather his wood, and build his fire. He has nothing to do but to wait for the next fight, and to make the time pass as best he can. In camp the burghers are like a party of children. They play games with each other, and play tricks upon each other, and engage in numerous wrestling bouts, a form of contest of which they seem particularly fond. They are like children also in that they are direct and simple, and as courteous as the ideal child should be. Indeed, if I were asked what struck me as the chief characteristics of the Boer I should say they were the two qualities which the English have always disallowed him, his simplicity rather than his "cuteness," and his courtesy rather than his boorishness.

The force that waited at the drift by Cronje's farm as it lay spread out on both sides of the river looked like a gathering of Wisconsin lumbermen, of Adirondack guides and hunters halted at Paul Smith's, like a Methodist camp-meeting limited entirely to men.

The eye sought in vain for rows of tents, for the horses at the picket line, for the flags that marked the headquarters, the commissariat, the field telegraph, the field post-office, the A. S. C., the R. M. A. C., the C. O., and all the other combinations of letters of the military alphabet.

I remembered that great army of General Buller's as I saw it stretching out over the basin of the Tugela, like the children of Israel in number, like Tammany Hall in organization and discipline, with not a tent-pin missing; with hospitals as complete as those established for a hundred years in the heart of London; with search-lights, heliographs, war balloons, Roentgen rays, pontoon bridges, telegraph wagons, and trenching tools, farriers with anvils, major-generals, mapmakers, "gallopers," intelligence departments, even biographs and press-censors; every kind of thing and every kind of man that goes to make up a British army corps. I knew that seven miles from us just such another completely equipped and disciplined column was advancing to the opposite bank of the Sand River.

And opposed to it was this merry company of Boer farmers lying on the grass, toasting pieces of freshly killed ox on the end of a stick, their hobbled ponies foraging for themselves a half-mile away, a thousand men without a tent among them, without a field-glass.

It was a picnic, a pastoral scene, not a scene of war. On the hills overlooking the drift were the guns, but down along the banks the burghers were sitting in circles singing the evening hymns, many of them sung to the tunes familiar in the service of the Episcopal Church, so that it sounded like a Sunday evening in the country at home. At the drift other burghers were watering the oxen, bathing and washing in the cold river; around the camp-fires others were smoking luxuriously, with their saddles for pillows. The evening breeze brought the sweet smell of burning wood, a haze of smoke from many fires, the lazy hum of hundreds of voices rising in the open air, the neighing of many horses, and the swift soothing rush of the river.

When morning came to Cronje's farm it brought with it no warning nor sign of battle. We began to believe that the British army was an invention of the enemy's. So we cooked bacon and fed the doves, and smoked on the veranda, moving our chairs around it with the sun, and argued as to whether we should stay where we were or go on to the bridge. At noon it was evident there would be no fight at the drift that day, so we started along the bank of the river, with the idea of reaching the bridge before nightfall. The trail lay on the English side of the river, so that we were in constant concern lest our white-hooded Cape cart would be seen by some of their scouts and we would be taken prisoners and forced to travel all the way back to Cape Town. We saw many herds of deer, but no scouts or lancers, and, such being the effect of many kopjes, lost all ideas as to where we were. We knew we were bearing steadily south toward Lord Roberts, who as we later learned, was then some three miles distant.

About two o'clock his guns opened on our left, so we at least knew that we were still on the wrong side of the river and that we must be between the Boer and the English artillery. Except for that, our knowledge of our geographical position was a blank, and we accordingly "out-spanned" and cooked more bacon. "Outspanning" is unharnessing the ponies and mules and turning them out graze, and takes three minutes - "inspanning" is trying to catch them again, and takes from three to five hours.

We started back over the trail over which we had

come, and just at sunset saw a man appear from behind a rock and disappear again. Whether he was Boer or Briton I could not tell, but while I was examining the rock with my glasses two Boers came galloping forward and ordered me to "hands up." To sit with both arms in the air is an extremely ignominious position, and especially annoying if the pony is restless, so I compromised by waving my whip as high as I could reach with one hand, and still held in the horse with the other. The third man from behind the rock rode up at the same time. They said they had watched us coming from the English lines, and that we were prisoners. We assured them that for us nothing could be more satisfactory, because we now knew where we were, and because they had probably saved us a week's trip to Cape Town. They examined and approved of our credentials, and showed us the proper trail which we managed to follow until they had disappeared, when the trail disappeared also, and we were again lost in what seemed an interminable valley. But just before nightfall the fires of the commando showed in front of us and we rode into the camp of General Christian De Wet. He told us we could not reach the bridge that night, and showed us a farm-house on a distant kopje where we could find a place to spread our blankets. I was extremely glad to meet him, as he and General Botha are the most able and brave of the Boer generals. He was big, manly, and of impressive size, and, although he speaks English, he dictated to his adjutant many long and Old-World compliments to the Greater Republic across the seas.

We found the people in the farm-house on the distant kopje quite hysterical over the near presence of the British, and the entire place in such an uproar that we slept out in the veldt. In the morning we were awakened by the sound of the Vickar-Maxim or the "pom-pom" as the English call it, or "bomb-Maxim" as the Boers call it. By any name it was a remarkable gun and the most demoralizing of any of the smaller pieces which have been used in this campaign. One of its values is that its projectiles throw up sufficient dust to enable the gunner to tell exactly where they strike, and within a few seconds he is able to alter the range accordingly. In this way it is its own range-finder. Its bark is almost as dangerous as its bite, for its reports have a brisk, insolent sound like a postman's knock, or a cooper hammering rapidly on an empty keg, and there is an unexplainable mocking sound to the reports, as though the gun were laughing at you. The English Tommies used to call it very aptly the "hyena gun." I found it much less offensive from the rear than when I was with the British, and in front of it.

From the top of a kopje we saw that the battle had at last begun and that the bridge was the objective point. The English came up in great lines and blocks and from so far away and in such close order that at first in spite of the khaki they looked as though they wore uniforms of blue. They advanced steadily, and two hours later when we had ridden to a kopje still nearer the bridge, they were apparently in the same formation as when we had first seen them, only now farms that had lain far in their rear were overrun by them and they encompassed the whole basin. An army of twenty-five thousand men advancing in full view across a great plain appeals to you as something entirely lacking in the human element. You do not think of it as a collection of very tired, dusty, and perspiring men with aching legs and parched lips, but as an unnatural phenomenon, or a gigantic monster which wipes out a railway station, a cornfield, and a village with a single clutch of one of its tentacles. You would as soon attribute human qualities to a plague, a tidal wave, or a slowly slipping landslide. One of the tentacles composed of six thousand horse had detached itself and crossed the river below the bridge, where it was creeping up on Botha's right. We could see the burghers galloping before it toward Ventersburg. At the bridge General Botha and President Steyn stood in the open road and with uplifted arms waved the Boers back, calling upon them to stand. But the burghers only shook their heads and with averted eyes grimly and silently rode by them on the other side. They knew they were flanked, they knew the men in the moving mass in front of them were in the proportion of nine to one.

When you looked down upon the lines of the English army advancing for three miles across the plain, one could hardly blame them. The burghers did not even raise their Mausers. One bullet, the size of a broken slate-pencil, falling into a block three miles across and a mile deep, seems so inadequate. It was like trying to turn back the waves of the sea with a blow-pipe.

It is true they had held back as many at Colenso, but the defensive positions there were magnificent, and since then six months had passed, during which time the same thirty thousand men who had been fighting then were fighting still, while the enemy was always new, with fresh recruits and re-enforcements arriving daily.

As the English officers at Durban, who had so lately arrived from home that they wore swords, used to say with the proud consciousness of two hundred thousand men back of them: "It won't last much longer now. The

Boers have had their belly full of fighting. They're fed up on it; that's what it is; they're fed up."

They forgot that the Boers, who for three months had held Buller back at the Tugela, were the same Boers who were rushed across the Free State to rescue Cronje from Roberts, and who were then sent to meet the relief column at Fourteen Streams, and were then ordered back again to harass Roberts at Sannahspost, and who, at last, worn out, stale, heartsick, and hopeless at the unequal odds and endless fighting, fell back at Sand River.

For three months thirty thousand men had been attempting the impossible task of endeavoring to meet an equal number of the enemy in three different places at the same time.

I have seen a retreat in Greece when the men, before they left the trenches, stood up in them and raged and cursed at the advancing Turk, cursed at their government, at their king, at each other, and retreated with shame in their faces because they did so.

But the retreat of the burghers of the Free State was not like that. They rose one by one and saddled their ponies, with the look in their faces of men who had been attending the funeral of a friend and who were leaving just before the coffin was swallowed in the grave. Some of them, for a long time after the greater number of the commando had ridden away, sat upon the rocks staring down into the sunny valley below them, talking together gravely, rising to take a last look at the territory which was their own. The shells of the victorious British sang triumphantly over the heads of their own artillery, bursting impotently in white smoke or tearing up the veldt in fountains of dust.

But they did not heed them. They did not even send a revengeful bullet into the approaching masses. The sweetness of revenge could not pay for what they had lost. They looked down upon the farm-houses of men they knew; upon their own farm-houses rising in smoke; they saw the Englishmen like a pest of locusts settling down around gardens and farm-houses still nearer, and swallowing them up.

Their companions, already far on the way to safety, waved to them from the veldt to follow; an excited doctor carrying a wounded man warned us that the English were just below, storming the hill. "Our artillery is aiming at five hundred yards," he shouted, but still the remaining burghers stood immovable, leaning on their rifles, silent, homeless, looking down without rage or show of feeling at the great waves of khaki sweeping steadily toward them, and possessing their land.

THE JAPANESE-RUSSIAN WAR:

BATTLES I DID NOT SEE

We knew it was a battle because the Japanese officers told us it was. In other wars I had seen other battles, many sorts of battles, but I had never seen a battle like that one. Most battles are noisy, hurried, and violent, giving rise to an unnatural thirst and to the delusion that, by some unhappy coincidence, every man on the other side is shooting only at you. This delusion is not peculiar to myself. Many men have told me that in the confusion of battle they always get this exaggerated idea of their own importance. Down in Cuba I heard a colonel inform a group of brother officers that a Spanish field-piece had marked him for its own, and for an hour had been pumping shrapnel at him and at no one else. The interesting part of the story was that he believed it.

But the battle of Anshantien was in no way disquieting. It was a noiseless, odorless, rubber-tired battle. So far as we were concerned it consisted of rings of shrapnel smoke floating over a mountain pass many miles distant. So many miles distant that when, with a glass, you could see a speck of fire twinkle in the sun like a heliograph, you could not tell whether it was the flash from the gun or the flame from the shell. Neither could you tell whether the cigarette rings issued from the lips of the Japanese guns or from those of the Russians. The only thing about that battle of which you were certain was that it was a perfectly safe battle to watch. It was the first one I ever witnessed that did not require you to calmly smoke a pipe in order to conceal the fact that you were scared. But soothing as it was, the battle lacked what is called the human interest. There may have been men behind the guns, but as they were also behind Camel Hill and Saddle Mountain, eight miles away, our eyes, like those of Mr. Samuel Weller, "being only eyes," were not able to discover them.

Our teachers, the three Japanese officers who were detailed to tell us about things we were not allowed to see, gazed at the scene of carnage with well-simulated horror. Their expressions of countenance showed that should any one move the battle eight miles nearer, they were prepared to sell their lives dearly. When they found that none of us were looking at them or their battle, they were hurt. The reason no one was looking at them was because most of us had gone to sleep. The rest, with a bitter experience of Japanese promises, had doubted there would be a battle, and had prepared themselves with newspapers. And so, while eight miles away the preliminary battle to Liao-Yang was making history, we were lying on the grass reading two months' old news of the St. Louis Convention.

The sight greatly disturbed our teachers.

"You complain," they said, "because you are not allowed to see anything, and now, when we show you a battle, you will not look."

Lewis, of the Herald, eagerly seized his glasses and

followed the track of the Siberian railway as it disappeared into the pass.

"I beg your pardon, but I didn't know it was a battle," he apologized politely. "I thought it was a locomotive at Anshantien Station blowing off steam."

And, so, teacher gave him a bad mark for disrespect.

It really was trying.

In order to see this battle we had travelled half around the world, had then waited four wasted months at Tokio, then had taken a sea voyage of ten days, then for twelve days had ridden through mud and dust in pursuit of the army, then for twelve more days, while battles raged ten miles away, had been kept prisoners in a compound where five out of the eighteen correspondents were sick with dysentery or fever, and finally as a reward we were released from captivity and taken to see smoke rings eight miles away! That night a round-robin, which was signed by all, was sent to General Oku, pointing out to him that unless we were allowed nearer to his army than eight miles, our usefulness to the people who paid us our salaries was at an end.

While waiting for an answer to this we were led out to see another battle. Either that we might not miss one minute of it, or that we should be too sleepy to see anything of it, we were started in black darkness, at three o'clock in the morning, the hour, as we are told, when one's vitality is at its lowest, and one which should be reserved for the exclusive use of burglars and robbers of hen roosts. Concerning that hour I learned this, that whatever its effects may be upon human beings, it finds a horse at his most strenuous moment. At that hour by the light of three paper lanterns we tried to saddle eighteen horses, donkeys, and ponies, and the sole object of each was to kick the light out of the lantern nearest him. We finally rode off through a darkness that was lightened only by a gray, dripping fog, and in a silence broken only by the patter of rain upon the corn that towered high above our heads and for many miles hemmed us in. After an hour, Sataki, the teacher who acted as our guide, lost the trail and Captain Lionel James, of the Times, who wrote "On the Heels of De Wet," found it for him. Sataki, so our two other keepers told us, is an authority on international law, and he may be all of that and know all there is to know of three-mile limits and paper blockades, but when it came to picking up a trail, even in the bright sunlight when it lay weltering beneath his horse's nostrils, we always found that any correspondent with an experience of a few campaigns was of more general use. The trail ended at a muddy hill, a bare sugar-loaf of a hill, as high as the main tent of a circus and as abruptly sloping away. It was swept by a damp, chilling wind; a mean, peevish rain washed its sides, and they were so steep that if we sat upon them we tobogganed slowly downward, ploughing up the mud with our boot heels. Hungry, sleepy, in utter darkness, we clung to this slippery mound in its ocean of whispering millet like sailors wrecked in mid-sea upon a rock, and waited for the day. After two hours a gray mist came grudgingly, trees and rocks grew out of it, trenches appeared at our feet, and what had before looked like a lake of water became a mud village.

Then, like shadows, the foreign attaches, whom we fondly hoped might turn out to be Russian Cossacks coming to take us prisoners and carry us off to breakfast, rode up in silence and were halted at the base of the hill. It seemed now, the audience being assembled, the orchestra might begin. But no hot-throated cannon broke the chilling, dripping, silence, no upheaval of the air spoke of Canet guns, no whirling shrapnel screamed and burst. Instead, the fog rolled back showing us miles of waving corn, the wet rails of the Siberian Railroad glistening in the rain, and, masking the horizon, the same mountains from which the day before the smoke rings had ascended. They now were dark, brooding, their tops hooded in clouds. Somewhere in front of us hidden in the Kiao liang, hidden in the tiny villages, crouching on the banks of streams, concealed in trenches that were themselves concealed, Oku's army, the army to which we were supposed to belong, was buried from our sight. And in the mountains on our right lay the Fourth Army, and twenty miles still farther to the right, Kuroki was closing in upon Liao-Yang. All of this we guessed, what we were told was very different, what we saw was nothing. In all, four hundred thousand men were not farther from us than four to thirty miles - and we saw nothing. We watched as the commissariat wagons carrying food to these men passed us by, the hospital stores passed us by, the transport carts passed us by, the coolies with reserve mounts, the last wounded soldier, straggler, and camp-follower passed us by. Like a big tidal wave Oku's army had swept forward leaving its unwelcome guests, the attaches and correspondents, forty lonely foreigners among seventy thousand Japanese, stranded upon a hill miles in the rear. Perhaps, as war, it was necessary, but it was not magnificent.

That night Major Okabe, our head teacher, gave us the official interpretation of what had occurred. The

Russians, he said, had retreated from Liao-Yang and were in open flight. Unless General Kuroki, who, he said, was fifty miles north of us, could cut them off they would reach Mukden in ten days, and until then there would be no more fighting. The Japanese troops, he said, were in Liao-Yang, it had been abandoned without a fight. This he told us on the evening of the 27th of August.

The next morning Major Okabe delivered the answer of General Oku to our round-robin. He informed us that we had been as near to the fighting as we ever would be allowed to go. The nearest we had been to any fighting was four miles. Our experience had taught us that when the Japanese promised us we would be allowed to do something we wanted to do, they did not keep their promise; but that when they said we would not be allowed to do something we wanted to do, they spoke the truth. Consequently, when General Oku declared the correspondents would be held four miles in the rear, we believed he would keep his word. And, as we now know, he did, the only men who saw the fighting that later ensued being those who disobeyed his orders and escaped from their keepers. Those who had been ordered by their papers to strictly obey the regulations of the Japanese, and the military attaches, were kept by Oku nearly six miles in the rear.

On the receipt of Oku's answer to the correspondents, Mr. John Fox, Jr., of Scribner's Magazine, Mr. Milton Prior, of the London Illustrated News, Mr. George Lynch, of the London Morning Chronicle, and myself left the army. We were very sorry to go. Apart from the fact that we had not been allowed to see anything of the military operations, we were enjoying ourselves immensely. Personally, I never went on a campaign in a more delightful country nor with better companions than the men acting as correspondents with the Second Army. For the sake of such good company, and to see more of Manchuria, I personally wanted to keep on. But I was not being paid to go camping with a set of good fellows. Already the Japanese had wasted six months of my time and six months of Mr. Collier's money, Mr. Fox had been bottled up for a period of equal length, while Mr. Prior and Mr. Lynch had been prisoners in Tokio for even four months longer. And now that Okabe assured us that Liao-Yang was already taken, and Oku told us if there were any fighting we would not be allowed to witness it, it seemed a good time to quit.

Other correspondents would have quit then, as most of them did ten days later, but that their work and ours in a slight degree differed. As we were not working for daily papers, we used the cable but seldom, while they used it every day. Each evening Okabe brought them the official account of battles and of the movements of the troops, which news of events which they had not witnessed they sent to their separate papers. But for our purposes it was necessary we should see things for ourselves. For, contrary to the popular accusation, no matter how flattering it may be, we could not describe events at which we were not present.

But what mainly moved us to decide, was the statements of Okabe, the officer especially detailed by the War Office to aid and instruct us, to act as our guide, philosopher, and friend, our only official source of information, who told us that Liao-Yang was occupied by the Japanese and that the Russians were in retreat. He even begged me personally to come with him into Liao-Yang on the 29th and see how it was progressing under the control of the Japanese authorities.

Okabe's news meant that the great battle Kuropatkin had promised at Liao-Yang, and which we had come to see, would never take place.

Why Okabe lied I do not know. Whether Oku had lied to him, or whether it was Baron-General Kodama or Major-General Fukushima who had instructed him to so grossly misinform us, it is impossible to say. While in Tokio no one ever more frequently, nor more unblushingly, made statements that they knew were untrue than did Kodama and Fukushima, but none of their deceptions had ever harmed us so greatly as did the lie they put into the mouth of Okabe. Not only had the Japanese NOT occupied Liao-Yang on the evening of the 27th of August, but later, as everybody knows, they had TO FIGHT SIX DAYS to get into it. And Kuroki, so far from being fifty miles north toward Mukden as Okabe said he was, was twenty miles to the east on our right preparing for the closing in movement which was just about to begin. Three days after we had left the army, the greatest battle since Sedan was waged for six days.

So our half year of time and money, of dreary waiting, of daily humiliations at the hands of officers with minds diseased by suspicion, all of which would have been made up to us by the sight of this one great spectacle, was to the end absolutely lost to us. Perhaps we made a mistake in judgment. As the cards fell, we certainly did. But after the event it is easy to be wise. For the last fifteen years, had I known as much the night before the Grand Prix was run as I did the next afternoon, I would be passing rich.

The only proposition before us was this: There was small chance of any immediate fighting. If there were fighting we could not see it. Confronted with the same conditions again, I would decide in exactly the same manner. Our misfortune lay in the fact that our experience with other armies had led us to believe that officers and gentlemen speak the truth, that men with titles of nobility, and with the higher titles of general and major-general, do not lie. In that we were mistaken.

The parting from the other correspondents was a brutal attack upon the feelings which, had we known they were to follow us two weeks later to Tokio, would have been spared us. It is worth recording why, after waiting many months to get to the front, they in their turn so soon left it. After each of the big battles before Liao-Yang they handed the despatches they had written for their papers to Major Okabe. Each day he told them these despatches had been censored and forwarded. After three days he brought back all the despatches and calmly informed the correspondents that not one of their cables had been sent. It was the final affront of Japanese duplicity. In recording the greatest battle of modern times three days had been lost, and by a lie. The object of their coming to the Far East had been frustrated. It was fatuous to longer expect from Kodama and his pupils fair play or honest treatment, and in the interest of their employers and to save their own self-respect, the representatives of all the most important papers in the world, the Times, of London, the New York Herald, the Paris Figaro, the London Daily Telegraph, Daily Mail, and Morning Post, quit the Japanese army.

Meanwhile, unconscious of what we had missed, the

four of us were congratulating ourselves upon our escape, and had started for New-Chwang. Our first halt was at Hai-Cheng, in the same compound in which for many days with the others we had been imprisoned. But our halt was a brief one. We found the compound glaring in the sun, empty, silent, filled only with memories of the men who, with their laughter, their stories, and their songs had made it live.

But now all were gone, the old familiar faces and the familiar voices, and we threw our things back on the carts and hurried away. The trails between Hai-Cheng and the sea made the worst going we had encountered in Manchuria. You soon are convinced that the time has not been long since this tract of land lay entirely under the waters of the Gulf of Liaotung. You soon scent the salt air, and as you flounder in the alluvial deposits of ages, you expect to find the salt-water at the very roots of the millet. Water lies in every furrow of the miles of cornfields, water flows in streams in the roads, water spreads in lakes over the compounds, it oozes from beneath the very walls of the go-downs. You would not be surprised at any moment to see the tide returning to envelop you. In this liquid mud a cart can make a trail by the simple process of continuing forward. The havoc is created in the millet and the ditches its iron-studded wheels dig in the mud leave to the eyes of the next comer as perfectly good a trail as the one that has been in use for many centuries. Consequently the opportunities for choosing the wrong trail are excellent, and we embraced every opportunity. But friendly Chinamen, and certainly they are a friendly, human people, again and again cheerfully went far out of their way to guide us back to ours, and so, after two days, we found ourselves five miles from New-Chwang.

Here we agreed to separate. We had heard a marvellous tale that at New-Chwang there was ice, champagne, and a hotel with enamelled bath- tubs. We had unceasingly discussed the probability of this being true, and what we would do with these luxuries if we got them, and when we came so near to where they were supposed to be, it was agreed that one of us would ride on ahead and command them, while the others followed with the carts. The lucky number fell to John Fox, and he left us at a gallop. He was to engage rooms for the four, and to arrange for the care of seven Japanese interpreters and servants, nine Chinese coolies, and nineteen horses and mules. We expected that by eight o'clock we would be eating the best dinner John Fox could order. We were mistaken. Not that John Fox had not ordered the dinner, but no one ate it but John Fox. The very minute he left us Priory's cart turned turtle in the mud, and the largest of his four mules lay down in it and knocked off work. The mule was hot and very tired, and the mud was soft, cool, and wet, so he burrowed under its protecting surface until all we could see of him was his ears. The coolies shrieked at him, Prior issued ultimatums at him, the Japanese servants stood on dry land fifteen feet away and talked about him, but he only snuggled deeper into his mud bath. When there is no more of a mule to hit than his ears, he has you at a great disadvantage, and when the coolies waded in and tugged at his head, we found that the harder they tugged, the deeper they sank. When they were so far out of sight that we were in danger of losing them too, we ordered them to give up the struggle and unload the cart. Before we got it out of dry-dock, reloaded, and again in line with the other carts it was nine o clock, and dark.

In the meantime, Lynch, his sense of duty weakened by visions of enamelled bathtubs filled with champagne and floating lumps of ice, had secretly abandoned us, stealing away in the night and leaving us to follow. This, not ten minutes after we had started, Mr. Prior decided that he would not do, so he camped out with the carts in a village, while, dinnerless, supperless, and thirsty, I rode on alone. I reached New-Chwang at midnight, and after being refused admittance by the Japanese soldiers, was finally rescued by the Number One man from the Manchuria Hotel, who had been sent out by Fox with two sikhs and a lantern to find me. For some minutes I dared not ask him the fateful questions. It was better still to hope than to put one's fortunes to the test. But I finally summoned my courage.

"Ice, have got?" I begged.

"Have got," he answered.

There was a long, grateful pause, and then in a voice that trembled, I again asked, "Champagne, have got?"

Number One man nodded.

"Have got," he said.

I totally forgot until the next morning to ask about the enamelled bathtubs.

When I arrived John Fox had gone to bed, and as it was six weeks since any of us had seen a real bed, I did not wake him. Hence, he did not know I was in the hotel, and throughout the troubles that followed I slept soundly.

Meanwhile, Lynch, as a punishment for running away from us, lost his own way, and, after stumbling into an old sow and her litter of pigs, which on a dark night is enough to startle any one, stumbled into a Japanese outpost, was hailed as a Russian spy, and made prisoner. This had one advantage, as he now was able to find New-Chwang, to which place he was marched, closely guarded, arriving there at half-past two in the morning. Since he ran away from us he had been wandering about on foot for ten hours. He sent a note to Mr. Little, the British Consul, and to Bush Brothers, the kings of New-Chwang, and, still tormented by visions of ice and champagne, demanded that his captors take him to the Manchuria Hotel. There he swore they would find a pass from Fukushima allowing him to enter New-Chwang, three friends who could identify him, four carts, seven servants, nine coolies, and nineteen animals. The commandant took him to the Manchuria Hotel, where instead of this wealth of corroborative detail they found John Fox in bed. As Prior, the only one of us not in New-Chwang, had the pass from Fukushima, permitting us to enter it, there was no one to prove what either Lynch or Fox said, and the officer flew into a passion and told Fox he would send both of them out of town on the first train. Mr. Fox was annoyed at being pulled from his bed at three in the morning to be told he was a Russian spy, so he said that there was not a train fast enough to get him out of New-Chwang as quickly as he wanted to go, or, for that matter, out of Japan and away from the Japanese people. At this the officer, being a Yale graduate, and speaking very pure English, told Mr. Fox to "shut up," and Mr. Fox being a Harvard graduate, with an equally perfect command of English, pure and undefiled, shook his fist in the face of the Japanese officer and told him to "shut up yourself." Lynch, seeing the witness he had summoned for the defence about to plunge into conflict with his captor, leaped unhappily from foot to foot, and was heard diplomatically suggesting that all hands should adjourn for ice and champagne.

"If I were a spy," demanded Fox, "do you suppose I would have ridden into your town on a white horse and registered at your head-quarters and then ordered four rooms at the principal hotel and accommodations for seven servants, nine coolies, and nineteen animals? Is that the way a Russian spy works? Does he go around with a brass band?"

The officer, unable to answer in kind this excellent reasoning, took a mean advantage of his position by placing both John and Lynch under arrest, and at the head of each bed a Japanese policeman to guard their slumbers. The next morning Prior arrived with the pass, and from the decks of the first out-bound English steamer Fox hurled through the captain's brass speaking-trumpet our farewells to the Japanese, as represented by the gun-boats in the harbor. Their officers, probably thinking his remarks referred to floating mines, ran eagerly to the side. But our ship's captain tumbled from the bridge, rescued his trumpet, and begged Fox, until we were under the guns of a British man-of-war, to issue no more farewell addresses. The next evening we passed into the Gulf of Pe-chi-li, and saw above Port Arthur the great guns flashing in the night, and the next day we anchored in the snug harbor of Chefoo.

I went at once to the cable station to cable Collier's I was returning, and asked the Chinaman in charge if my name was on his list of those correspondents who could send copy collect. He said it was; and as I started to write, he added with grave politeness, "I congratulate you."

For a moment I did not lift my eyes. I felt a chill creeping down my spine. I knew what sort of a blow was coming, and I was afraid of it.

"Why?" I asked.

The Chinaman bowed and smiled.

"Because you are the first," he said. "You are the only correspondent to arrive who has seen the battle of Liao-Yang."

The chill turned to a sort of nausea. I knew then what disaster had fallen, but I cheated myself by pretending the man was misinformed. "There was no battle," I protested. "The Japanese told me themselves they had entered Liao-Yang without firing a shot." The cable operator was a gentleman. He saw my distress, saw what it meant and delivered the blow with the distaste of a physician who must tell a patient he cannot recover. Gently, reluctantly, with real sympathy he said, "They have been fighting for six days."

I went over to a bench, and sat down; and when Lynch and Fox came in and took one look at me, they guessed what had happened. When the Chinaman told them of what we had been cheated, they, in their turn, came to the bench, and collapsed. No one said anything. No one even swore. Six months we had waited only to miss by three days the greatest battle since Gettysburg and Sedan. And by a lie.

For six months we had tasted all the indignities of the suspected spy, we had been prisoners of war, we had been ticket-of-leave men, and it is not difficult to imagine our glad surprise that same day when we saw in the harbor the white hull of the cruiser Cincinnati with our flag lifting at her stern. We did not know a soul on board, but that did not halt us. As refugees, as fleeing political prisoners, as American slaves escaping from their Japanese jailers, we climbed over the side and demanded protection and dinner. We got both. Perhaps it was not good to rest on that bit of driftwood, that atom of our country that had floated far from the mainland and now formed an island of American territory in the harbor of Chefoo. Perhaps we were not content to sit at the mahogany table in the glistening white and brass bound wardroom surrounded by those eager, sunburned faces, to hear sea slang and home slang in the accents of Maine, Virginia, and New York City. We forgot our dark-skinned keepers with the slanting, suspicious, unfriendly eyes, with tongues that spoke the one thing and meant the other. All the memories of those six months of deceit, of broken pledges, of unnecessary humiliations, of petty unpoliteness from a half-educated, half-bred, conceited, and arrogant people fell from us like a heavy knapsack. We were again at home. Again with our own people. Out of the happy confusion of that great occasion I recall two toasts. One was offered by John Fox. "Japan for the Japanese, and the Japanese for Japan." Even the Japanese wardroom boy did not catch its significance. The other was a paraphrase of a couplet in reference to our brown brothers of the Philippines first spoken in Manila. "To the Japanese: 'They may be brothers to Commodore Perry, but they ain't no brothers of mine.'"

It was a joyous night. Lieutenant Gilmore, who had been an historic prisoner in the Philippines, so far sympathized with our escape from the Yellow Peril as to intercede with the captain to extend the rules of the ship. And those rules that were incapable of extending broke. Indeed, I believe we broke everything but the eight-inch gun. And finally we were conducted to our steamer in a launch crowded with slim-waisted, broad-chested youths in white mess jackets, clasping each other's shoulders and singing, "Way down in my heart, I have a feeling for you, a sort of feeling for you"; while the officer of the deck turned his back, and discreetly fixed his night glass upon a suspicious star.

It was an American cruiser that rescued this war correspondent from the bondage of Japan. It will require all the battle-ships in the Japanese navy to force him back to it.

A WAR CORRESPONDENT'S KIT

I am going to try to describe some kits and outfits I have seen used in different parts of the world by travellers and explorers, and in different campaigns by army officers and war correspondents. Among the articles, the reader may learn of some new thing which, when next he goes hunting, fishing, or exploring, he can adapt to his own uses. That is my hope, but I am sceptical. I have seldom met the man who would allow any one else to select his kit, or who would admit that any other kit was better than the one he himself had packed. It is a very delicate question. The same article that one declares is the most essential to his comfort, is the very first thing that another will throw into the trail. A man's outfit is a matter which seems to touch his private honor. I have heard veterans sitting around a camp-fire proclaim the superiority of their kits with a jealousy, loyalty, and enthusiasm they would not exhibit for the flesh of their flesh and the bone of their bone. On a campaign, you may attack a man's courage, the flag he serves, the newspaper for which he works, his intelligence, or his camp manners, and he will ignore you; but if you criticise his patent water-bottle he will fall upon you with both fists. So, in recommending any article for an outfit, one needs to be careful. An outfit lends itself to dispute, because the selection of its component parts is not an exact science. It should be, but it is not. A doctor on his daily rounds can carry in a compact little satchel almost everything he is liable to need; a carpenter can stow away in one box all the tools of his trade. But an outfit is not selected on any recognized principles. It seems to be a question entirely of temperament. As the man said when his friends asked him how he made his famous cocktail, "It depends on my mood." The truth is that each man in selecting his outfit generally follows the lines of least resistance. With one, the pleasure he derives from his morning bath outweighs the fact that for the rest of the day he must carry a rubber bathtub. Another man is hearty, tough, and inured to an out-of-door life. He can sleep on a pile of coal or standing on his head, and he naturally scorns to carry a bed. But another man, should he sleep all night on the ground, the next day would be of no use to himself, his regiment, or his newspaper. So he carries a folding cot and the more fortunate one of tougher fibre laughs at him. Another man says that the only way to campaign is to travel "light," and sets forth with rain-coat and field-glass. He honestly thinks that he travels light because his intelligence tells him it is the better way; but, as a matter of fact, he does so because he is lazy. Throughout the entire campaign he borrows from his friends, and with that camaraderie and unselfishness that never comes to the surface so strongly as when men are thrown together in camp, they lend him whatever he needs. When the war is over, he is the man who goes about saying: "Some of those fellows carried enough stuff to fill a moving van. Now, look what I did. I made the entire campaign on a toothbrush."

As a matter of fact, I have a sneaking admiration for the man who dares to borrow. His really is the part of wisdom. But at times he may lose himself in places where he can neither a borrower nor a lender be, and there are men so tenderly constituted that they cannot keep another man hungry while they use his coffee-pot. So it is well to take a few things with you - if only to lend them to the men who travel "light."

On hunting and campaigning trips the climate, the means of transport, and the chance along the road of obtaining food and fodder vary so greatly that it is not possible to map out an outfit which would serve equally well for each of them. What on one journey was your most precious possession on the next is a useless nuisance. On two trips I have packed a tent weighing, with the stakes, fifty pounds, which, as we slept in huts, I never once had occasion to open; while on other trips in countries that promised to be more or less settled, I had to always live under canvas, and sometimes broke camp twice a day.

In one war, in which I worked for an English paper, we travelled like major-generals. When that war started few thought it would last over six weeks, and many of the officers regarded it in the light of a picnic. In consequence, they mobilized as they never would have done had they foreseen what was to come, and the mess contractor grew rich furnishing, not only champagne, which in campaigns in fever countries has saved the life of many a good man, but cases of even port and burgundy, which never greatly helped any one. Later these mess supplies were turned over to the field-hospitals, but at the start every one travelled with more than he needed and more than the regulations allowed, and each correspondent was advised that if he represented a first-class paper and wished to "save his face" he had better travel in state. Those who did not, found the staff and censor less easy of access, and the means of obtaining information more difficult. But it was a nuisance. If, when a man halted at your tent, you could not stand him whiskey and sparklet soda, Egyptian cigarettes, compressed soup, canned meats, and marmalade, your paper was suspected of trying to do it "on the cheap," and not only of being mean, but, as this was a popular war, unpatriotic. When the army stripped down to work all this was discontinued, but at the start I believe there were carried with that column as many tins of tan-leather dressing as there were rifles. On that march my own outfit was as unwieldy as a gypsy's caravan. It consisted of an enormous cart, two oxen, three Basuto ponies, one Australian horse, three servants, and four hundred pounds of supplies and baggage. When it moved across the plain it looked as large as a Fall River boat. Later, when I joined the opposing army, and was not expected to maintain the dignity of a great London daily, I carried all my belongings strapped to my back, or to the back of my one pony, and I was quite as comfortable, clean, and content as I had been with the private car and the circus tent.

Throughout the Greek war, as there were no horses to be had for love or money, we walked, and I learned then that when one has to carry his own kit the number of things he can do without is extraordinary. While I marched with the army, offering my kingdom for a horse, I carried my outfit in saddle-bags thrown over my shoulder. And I think it must have been a good outfit, for I never bought anything to add to it or threw anything away. I submit that as a fair test of a kit.

Further on, should any reader care to know how for several months one may keep going with an outfit he can pack in two saddle-bags, I will give a list of the articles which in three campaigns I carried in mine.

Personally, I am for travelling "light," but at the very start one is confronted with the fact that what one man calls light to another savors of luxury. I call fifty pounds light; in Japan we each were allowed the officer's allowance of sixty-six pounds. Lord Wolseley, in his "Pocketbook," cuts down the officer's kit to forty pounds, while "Nessmut," of the Forest and Stream, claims that for a hunting trip, all one wants does not weigh over twenty-six pounds. It is very largely a question of compromise. You cannot eat your cake and have it. You cannot, under a tropical sun, throw away your blanket and when the night dew falls wrap it around you. And if, after a day of hard climbing or riding, you want to drop into a folding chair, to make room for it in your carry-all you must give up many other lesser things.

By travelling light I do not mean any lighter than the necessity demands. If there is transport at hand, a man is foolish not to avail himself of it. He is always foolish if he does not make things as easy for himself as possible. The tenderfoot will not agree with this. With him there is no idea so fixed, and no idea so absurd, as that to be comfortable is to be effeminate. He believes that "roughing it" is synonymous with hardship, and in season and out of season he plays the Spartan. Any man who suffers discomforts he can avoid because he fears his comrades will think he cannot suffer hardships is an idiot. You often hear it said of a man that "he can rough it with the best of them." Any one can do that. The man I want for a "bunkie" is the one who can be comfortable while the best of them are roughing it. The old soldier knows that it is his duty to keep himself fit, so that he can perform his work, whether his work is scouting for forage or scouting for men, but you will often hear the volunteer captain say: "Now, boys, don't forget we're roughing it; and don't expect to be comfortable." As a rule, the only reason his men are uncomfortable is because he does not know how to make them otherwise; or because he thinks, on a campaign, to endure unnecessary hardship is the mark of a soldier.

In the Cuban campaign the day the American forces landed at Siboney a major-general of volunteers took up his head-quarters in the house from which the Spanish commandant had just fled, and on the veranda of which Caspar Whitney and myself had found two hammocks and made ourselves at home. The Spaniard who had been left to guard the house courteously offered the major-general his choice of three bedrooms. They all were on the first floor and opened upon the veranda, and to the general's staff a tent could have been no easier of access. Obviously, it was the duty of the general to keep himself in good physical condition, to obtain as much sleep as possible, and to rest his great brain and his limbs cramped with ten days on shipboard. But in a tone of stern reproof he said, "No; I am campaigning now, and I have given up all luxuries." And with that he stretched a poncho on the hard boards of the veranda, where, while just a few feet from him the three beds and white mosquito nets gleamed invitingly, he tossed and turned. Besides being a silly spectacle, the sight of an old gentleman lying wide awake on his shoulder-blades was disturbing, and as the hours dragged on we repeatedly offered him our hammocks. But he fretfully persisted in his determination to be uncomfortable. And he was. The feelings of his unhappy staff, several of whom were officers of the regular army, who had to follow the example of their chief, were toward morning hardly loyal. Later, at the very moment the army moved up to the battle of San Juan this same major-general was relieved of his command on account of illness. Had he sensibly taken care of himself, when the moment came when he was needed, he would have been able to better serve his brigade and his country. In contrast to this pose is the conduct of the veteran hunter, or old soldier. When he gets into camp his first thought, after he has cared for his horse, is for his own comfort. He does not wolf down a cold supper and then spread his blanket wherever he happens to be standing. He knows that, especially at night, it is unfair to ask his stomach to digest cold rations. He knows that the warmth of his body is needed to help him to sleep soundly, not to fight chunks of canned meat. So, no matter how sleepy he may be, he takes the time to build a fire and boil a cup of tea or coffee. Its warmth aids digestion and saves his stomach from working overtime. Nor will he act on the theory that he is "so tired he can sleep anywhere." For a few hours the man who does that may sleep the sleep of exhaustion. But before day breaks he will feel under him the roots and stones, and when he awakes he is stiff, sore and unrefreshed. Ten minutes spent in digging holes for hips and shoulder-blades, in collecting grass and branches to spread beneath his blanket, and leaves to stuff in his boots for a pillow, will give him a whole night of comfort and start him well and fit on the next day's tramp. If you have watched an old sergeant, one of the Indian fighters, of which there are now too few left in the army, when he goes into camp, you will see him build a bunk and possibly a shelter of boughs just as though for the rest of his life he intended to dwell in that particular spot. Down in the Garcia campaign along the Rio Grande I said to one of them: "Why do you go to all that trouble? We break camp at daybreak." He said: "Do we? Well, maybe you know that, and maybe the captain knows that, but I don't know it. And so long as I don't know it, I am going to be just as snug as though I was halted here for a month." In camping, that was one of my first and best lessons - to make your surroundings healthy and comfortable. The temptation always is to say, "Oh, it is for only one night, and I am too tired." The next day you say the same thing, "We'll move to-morrow. What's the use?" But the fishing or shooting around the camp proves good, or it comes on to storm, and for maybe a week you do not move, and for a week you suffer discomforts. An hour of work put in at the beginning would have turned it into a week of ease.

When there is transport of even one pack-horse, one of the best helps toward making camp quickly is a combination of panniers and bed used for many years by E. F. Knight, the Times war correspondent, who lost an arm at Gras Pan. It consists of two leather trunks, which by day carry your belongings slung on either side of the pack-animal, and by night act as uprights for your bed. The bed is made of canvas stretched on two poles which rest on the two trunks. For travelling in upper India this arrangement is used almost universally. Mr. Knight obtained his during the Chitral campaign, and since then has used it in every war. He had it with Kuroki's army during this last campaign in Manchuria. {6}

A more compact form of valise and bed combined is the "carry-all," or any of the many makes of sleeping-bags, which during the day carry the kit and at night when spread upon the ground serve for a bed. The one once most used by Englishmen was Lord Wolseley's "valise and sleeping-bag." It was complicated by a number of strings, and required as much lacing as a dozen pairs of boots. It has been greatly improved by a new sleeping-bag with straps, and flaps that tuck in at the ends. But the obvious disadvantage of all sleeping-bags is that in rain and mud you are virtually lying on the hard ground, at the mercy of tarantula and fever.

The carry-all is, nevertheless, to my mind, the most nearly perfect way in which to pack a kit. I have tried the trunk, valise, and sleeping-bag, and vastly prefer it to them all. My carry-all differs only from the sleeping-bag in that, instead of lining it so that it may be used as a bed, I carry in its pocket a folding cot. By omitting the extra lining for the bed, I save almost the weight of the cot. The folding cot I pack is the Gold Medal Bed, made in this country, but which you can purchase almost anywhere. I once carried one from Chicago to Cape Town to find on arriving I could buy the bed there at exactly the same price I had paid for it in America. I also found them in Tokio, where imitations of them were being made by the ingenious and disingenuous Japanese. They are light in weight, strong, and comfortable, and are undoubtedly the best camp-bed made. When at your elevation of six inches above the ground you look down from one of them upon a comrade in a sleeping-bag with rivulets of rain and a tide of muddy water rising above him, your satisfaction, as you fall asleep, is worth the weight of the bed in gold.

My carry-all is of canvas with a back of waterproof. It is made up of three strips six and a half feet long. The two outer strips are each two feet three inches wide, the middle strip four feet. At one end of the middle strip is a deep pocket of heavy canvas with a flap that can be fastened by two straps. When the kit has been packed in this pocket, the two side strips are folded over it and the middle strip and the whole is rolled up and buckled by two heavy straps on the waterproof side. It is impossible for any article to fall out or for the rain to soak in. I have a smaller carry-all made on the same plan, but on a tiny scale, in which to carry small articles and a change of clothing. It goes into the pocket after the bed, chair, and the heavier articles are packed away. When the bag is rolled up they are on the outside of and form a protection to the articles of lighter weight.

The only objection to the carry-all is that it is an awkward bundle to pack. It is difficult to balance it on the back of an animal, but when you are taking a tent with you or carrying your provisions, it can be slung on one side of the pack saddle to offset their weight on the other.

I use the carry-all when I am travelling "heavy." By that I mean when it is possible to obtain pack-animal or cart. When travelling light and bivouacking by night without a pack-horse, bed, or tent, I use the saddle-bags, already described. These can be slung over the back of the horse you ride, or if you walk, carried over your shoulder. I carried them in this latter way in Greece, in the Transvaal, and Cuba during the rebellion, and later with our own army.

The list of articles I find most useful when travelling where it is possible to obtain transport, or, as we may call it, travelling heavy, are the following:

A tent, seven by ten feet, with fly, jointed poles, tent-pins, a heavy mallet. I recommend a tent open at both ends with a window cut in one end. The window, when that end is laced and the other open, furnishes a draught of air. The window should be covered with a flap which, in case of rain, can be tied down over it with tapes. A great convenience in a tent is a pocket sewn inside of each wall, for boots, books, and such small articles. The pocket should not be filled with anything so heavy as to cause the walls to sag. Another convenience with a tent is a leather strap stretched from pole to pole, upon which to hang clothes, and another is a strap to be buckled around the front tent-pole, and which is studded with projecting hooks for your lantern, water-bottle, and field-glasses. This latter can be bough ready-made at any military outfitter's.

Many men object to the wooden tent-pin on account of its tendency to split, and carry pins made of iron. With these, an inch below the head of the pin is a projecting barb which holds the tent rope. When the pin is being driven in, the barb is out of reach of the mallet. Any blacksmith can beat out such pins, and if you can afford the extra weight, they are better than those of ash. Also, if you can afford the weight, it is well to carry a strip of water-proof or oilcloth for the floor of the tent to keep out dampness. All these things appertaining to the tent should be tolled up in it, and the tent itself carried in a light-weight receptacle, with a running noose like a sailor's kit-bag.

The carry-all has already been described. Of its contents, I consider first in importance the folding bed.

And second in importance I would place a folding chair. Many men scoff at a chair as a cumbersome luxury. But after a hard day on foot or in the saddle, when you sit on the ground with your back to a rock and your hands locked across your knees to keep yourself from sliding, or on a box with no rest for your spinal column, you begin to think a chair is not a luxury, but a necessity. During the Cuban campaign, for a time I was a member of General Sumner's mess. The general owned a folding chair, and whenever his back was turned every one would make a rush to get into it. One time we were discussing what, in the light of our experience of that campaign, we would take with us on our next, and all agreed, Colonel Howze, Captain Andrews, and Major Harmon, that if one could only take one article it would be a chair. I carried one in Manchuria, but it was of no use to me, as the other correspondents occupied it, relieving each other like sentries on guard duty. I had to pin a sign on it, reading, "Don't sit on me," but no one ever saw the sign. Once, in order to rest in my own chair, I weakly established a precedent by giving George Lynch a cigar to allow me to sit down (on that march there was a mess contractor who supplied us even with cigars, and occasionally with food), and after that, whenever a man wanted to smoke, he would commandeer my chair, and unless bribed refuse to budge. This seems to argue the popularity of the contractor's cigars rather than that of the chair, but, nevertheless, I submit that on a campaign the article second in importance for rest, comfort, and content is a chair. The best I know is one invented by Major Elliott of the British army. I have an Elliott chair that I have used four years, not only when camping out, but in my writing-room at home. It is an arm-chair, and is as comfortable as any made. The objections to it are its weight, that it packs bulkily, and takes down into too many pieces. Even with these disadvantages it is the best chair. It can be purchased at the Army and Navy and Anglo-Indian stores in London. A chair of lighter weight and one-fourth the bulk is the Willisden chair, of green canvas and thin iron supports. It breaks in only two pieces, and is very comfortable.

Sir Harry Johnson, in his advice to explorers, makes a great point of their packing a chair. But he recommends one known as the "Wellington," which is a cane-bottomed affair, heavy and cumbersome. Dr. Harford, the instructor in outfit for the Royal Geographical Society, recommends a steamer-chair, because it can be used on shipboard and "can be easily carried afterward." If there be anything less easy to carry than a deck-chair I have not met it. One might as soon think of packing a folding step-ladder. But if he has the transport, the man who packs any reasonably light folding chair will not regret it.

As a rule, a cooking kit is built like every other cooking kit in that the utensils for cooking are carried in the same pot that is used for boiling the water, and the top of the pot turns itself into a frying-pan. For eight years I always have used the same kind of cooking kit, so I cannot speak of others with knowledge; but I have always looked with envious eyes at the Preston cooking kit and water-bottle. Why it has not already been adopted by every army I do not understand, for in no army have I seen a kit as compact or as light, or one that combines as many useful articles and takes up as little room. It is the invention of Captain Guy H. Preston, Thirteenth Cavalry, and can be purchased at any military outfitter's.

The cooking kit I carry is, or was, in use in the German army. It is made of aluminum, - weighs about as much as a cigarette-case, and takes up as little room as would a high hat. It is a frying-pan and coffee-pot combined.

From the Germans it has been borrowed by the Japanese, and one smaller than mine, but of the same pattern, is part of the equipment of each Japanese soldier. On a day's march there are three things a man must carry: his water-bottle, his food, which, with the soldier, is generally carried in a haversack, and his cooking kit. Preston has succeeded most ingeniously in combining the water-bottle and the cooking kit, and I believe by cutting his water-bottle in half, he can make room in his coffee-pot for the food. If he will do this, he will solve the problem of carrying water, food, and the utensils for cooking the food and for boiling the water in one receptacle, which can be carried from the shoulder by a single strap. The alteration I have made for my own use in Captain Preston's water-bottle enables me to carry in the coffee-pot one day's rations of bacon, coffee, and biscuit.

In Tokio, before leaving for Manchuria, General Fukushima asked me to bring my entire outfit to the office of the General Staff. I spread it out on the floor, and with unerring accuracy he selected from it the three articles of greatest value. They were the Gold Medal cot, the Elliott chair, and Preston's water-bottle. He asked if he could borrow these, and, understanding that he wanted to copy them for his own use, and supposing that if he used them, he would, of course, make some restitution to the officers who had invented them, I foolishly loaned them to him. Later, he issued them in numbers to the General Staff. As I felt, in a manner, responsible, I wrote to the Secretary of War, saying I was sure the Japanese army did not wish to benefit by these inventions without making some acknowledgment or return to the inventors. But the Japanese War Office could not see the point I tried to make, and the General Staff wrote a letter in reply asking why I had not directed my communication to General Fukushima, as it was not the Secretary of War, but he, who had taken the articles. The fact that they were being issued without any return being made, did not interest them. They passed cheerfully over the fact that the articles had been stolen, and were indignant, not because I had accused a Japanese general of pilfering, but because I had accused the wrong general. The letter was so insolent that I went to the General Staff Office and explained that the officer who wrote it, must withdraw it, and apologize for it. Both of which things he did. In case the gentlemen whose inventions were "borrowed" might, if they wished, take further steps in the matter, I sent the documents in the case, with the exception of the letter which was withdrawn, to the chief of the General Staff in the United States and in England.

In importance after the bed, cooking kit, and chair, I would place these articles:

Two collapsible water-buckets of rubber or canvas.
Two collapsible brass lanterns, with extra isinglass sides.
Two boxes of sick-room candles.
One dozen boxes of safety matches.
One axe. The best I have seen is the Marble Safety Axe, made at Gladstone, Mich. You can carry it in your hip-pocket, and you can cut down a tree with it.
One medicine case containing quinine, calomel, and Sun Cholera
Mixture in tablets.
Toilet-case for razors, tooth-powder, brushes, and paper.

Folding bath-tub of rubber in rubber case. These are manufactured to fold into a space little larger than a cigar-box.
Two towels old, and soft.
Three cakes of soap.
One Jaeger blanket.
One mosquito head-bag.
One extra pair of shoes, old and comfortable.
One extra pair of riding-breeches.
One extra pair of gaiters. The former regulation army gaiter of canvas, laced, rolls up in a small compass and weighs but little.
One flannel shirt. Gray least shows the dust.
Two pairs of drawers. For riding, the best are those of silk.
Two undershirts, balbriggan or woollen.
Three pairs of woollen socks.
Two linen handkerchiefs, large enough, if needed, to tie around the throat and protect the back of the neck.
One pair of pajamas, woollen, not linen.
One housewife.
Two briarwood pipes.
Six bags of smoking tobacco; Durham or Seal of North Carolina pack easily.
One pad of writing paper.
One fountain pen, SELF-FILLING.
One bottle of ink, with screw top, held tight by a spring.
One dozen linen envelopes.
Stamps, wrapped in oil-silk with mucilage side next to the silk.
One stick sealing-wax. In tropical countries mucilage on the flap of envelopes sticks to everything except the envelope.
One dozen elastic bands of the largest size. In packing they help to compress articles like clothing into the

smallest possible compass and in many other ways will be found very useful.
One pack of playing-cards.
Books.
One revolver and six cartridges.

The reason for most of these articles is obvious. Some of them may need a word of recommendation. I place the water-buckets first in the list for the reason that I have found them one of my most valuable assets. With one, as soon as you halt, instead of waiting for your turn at the well or water-hole, you can carry water to your horse, and one of them once filled and set in the shelter of the tent, later saves you many steps. It also can be used as a nose-bag, and to carry fodder. I recommend the brass folding lantern, because those I have tried of tin or aluminum have invariably broken. A lantern is an absolute necessity. When before daylight you break camp, or hurry out in a wind storm to struggle with flying tent-pegs, or when at night you wish to read or play cards, a lantern with a stout frame and steady light is indispensable. The original cost of the sick-room candles is more than that of ordinary candles, but they burn longer, are brighter, and take up much less room. To protect them and the matches from dampness, or the sun, it is well to carry them in a rubber sponge-bag. Any one who has forgotten to pack a towel will not need to be advised to take two. An old sergeant of Troop G, Third Cavalry, once told me that if he had to throw away everything he carried in his roll but one article, he would save his towel. And he was not a particularly fastidious sergeant either, but he preferred a damp towel in his roll to damp clothes on his back. Every man knows the dreary halts in camp when the rain pours outside, or the regiment is held in reserve. For times like these a pack of cards or a book is worth carrying, even if it weighs as much as the plates from which it was printed. At present it is easy to obtain all of the modern classics in volumes small enough to go into the coat-pocket. In Japan, before starting for China, we divided up among the correspondents Thomas Nelson & Sons' and Doubleday, Page & Co.'s pocket editions of Dickens, Thackeray, and Lever, and as most of our time in Manchuria was spent locked up in compounds, they proved a great blessing.

In the list I have included a revolver, following out the old saying that "You may not need it for a long time, but when you do need it, you want it damned quick." Except to impress guides and mule-drivers, it is not an essential article. In six campaigns I have carried one, and never used it, nor needed it but once, and then while I was dodging behind the foremast it lay under tons of luggage in the hold. The number of cartridges I have limited to six, on the theory that if in six shots you haven't hit the other fellow, he will have hit you, and you will not require another six.

This, I think, completes the list of articles that on different expeditions I either have found of use, or have seen render good service to some one else. But the really wise man will pack none of the things enumerated in this article. For the larger his kit, the less benefit he will have of it. It will all be taken from him. And accordingly my final advice is to go forth empty-handed, naked and unashamed, and borrow from your friends. I have never tried that method of collecting an outfit, but I have seen never it fail, and of all travellers the man who borrows is the wisest.

Footnotes:

{1} From "A Year from a Reporter's Note Book," copyright, 1897, by Harper & Brothers.

{2} From "A Year from a Reporter's Note Book, copyright, 1897, Harper & Brothers."

{3} For this "distinguished gallantry in action," James R. Church later received the medal of honor.

{4} Some of the names and initials on the trees are as follows: J. P. Allen; Lynch; Luke Steed; Happy Mack, Rough Riders; Russell; Ward; E. M. Lewis, C, 9th Cav.; Alex; E. K. T.; J. P. E.; W. N. D.; R. D. R.; I. W. S., 5th U. S.; J. M. B.; J. M. T., C, 9th.

{5} A price list during the siege:

SIEGE OF LADYSMITH,
1899-1900.

I certify that the following are the correct and highest prices realised at my sales by Public Auction during the above Siege,

JOE DYSON,
Auctioneer.

LADYSMITH,
FEBRUARY 21st, 1900.

	Pounds	s.	d.
14 lbs. Oatmeal	2	19	6
Condensed Milk, per tin	0	10	0
1 lb. Beef Fat	0	11	0
1 lb. Tin Coffee	0	17	0
2 lb. Tin Tongue	1	6	0
1 Sucking Pig	1	17	0
Eggs, per dozen	2	8	0
Fowls, each	0	18	6
4 Small Cucumbers	0	15	6
Green Mealies, each	0	3	8
Small plate Grapes	1	5	0
1 Small plate Apples	0	12	6
1 Plate Tomatoes	0	18	0
1 Vegetable Marrow	1	8	0
1 Plate Eschalots	0	11	0
1 Plate Potatoes	0	19	0
3 Small bunches Carrots	0	9	0
1 Glass Jelly	0	18	0
1 lb. Bottle Jam	1	11	0
1 lb. Tin Marmalade	1	1	0
1 dozen Matches	0	13	6
1 pkt. Cigarettes	1	5	0
50 Cigars	9	5	0
0.25 lb. Cake "Fair Maid" Tobacco	2	5	0
0.5 lb. Cake "Fair Maid"	3	5	0
1 lb. Sailors Tobacco	2	3	0
0.25 lb. tin "Capstan" Navy Cut Tobacco	3	0	0

{6} The top of the trunk is made of a single piece of leather with a rim that falls over the mouth of the trunk and protects the contents from rain. The two iron rings by which each box is slung across the padded back of the pack-horse are fastened by rivetted straps to the rear top line of each trunk. On both ENDS of each trunk near the top and back are two iron sockets. In these fit the staples that hold the poles for the bed. The staples are made of iron in the shape of the numeral 9, the poles passing through the circle of the 9. The bed should be four feet long three feet wide, of heavy canvas, strengthened by leather straps. At both ends are two buckles which connect with straps on the top of each trunk. Along one side of the canvas is a pocket running its length and open at both ends. Through this one of the poles passes and the other through a series of straps that extend on the opposite side. These straps can be shortened or tightened to allow a certain "give" to the canvas, which the ordinary stretcher-bed does not permit. The advantage of this arrangement is in the fact that it can be quickly put together and that it keeps the sleeper clear of the ground and safeguards him from colds and malaria.

www.ingramcontent.com/pod-product-compliance
Lightning Source LLC
Chambersburg PA
CBHW022358040426
42450CB00005B/239